RETURN OF THE JEDI

THE COMPLETE, FULLY ILLUSTRATED SCRIPT

GEORGE LUCAS AND LAWRENCE KASDAN

STORY BY GEORGE LUCAS

Virgin

First published by
Virgin Publishing Limited
Thames Wharf Studios
Rainville Road
London W6 9HT

ISBN 1 85227 729 7

Digiframe™ images produced directly from the movie by
Screenscene Ltd. Image selection and editing by Kevin
Reynolds, Screenscene Ltd.

Book design by DRi Design, Bath, England.

Colour Origination by Colourwise Ltd, W Sussex

Printed and bound in Great Britain by
Butler & Tanner Ltd, Frome and London.

A LONG TIME AGO IN A GALAXY FAR, FAR AWAY...

The boundless heavens serve as a backdrop
for the main title, followed by a roll-up,
which crawls into infinity.

STAR WARS
EPISODE VI
RETURN OF THE JEDI

Luke Skywalker has returned to
his home planet of Tatooine in
an attempt to rescue his
friend Han Solo from the
clutches of the vile gangster
Jabba the Hutt.

Little does Luke know that the
Galactic Empire has secretly
begun construction on a new
armored space station even
more powerful than the first
dreaded Death Star.

When completed, this ultimate
weapon will spell certain doom
for the small band of Rebels
struggling to restore
freedom to the galaxy...

PAN DOWN TO REVEAL A MONSTROUS HALF-COMPLETED DEATH STAR, ITS MASSIVE SUPERSTRUCTURE CURLING AWAY BEYOND THE COMPLETED SECTION LIKE THE ARMS OF A GIANT OCTOPUS.

AN IMPERIAL STAR DESTROYER MOVES OVERHEAD TOWARD THE MASSIVE ARMORED SPACE STATION, FOLLOWED BY TWO ZIPPING TIE FIGHTERS. A SMALL IMPERIAL SHUTTLE ROCKETS FROM THE MAIN BAY OF THE SHIP AND HUSTLES TOWARD THE DEATH STAR.

INTERIOR IMPERIAL SHUTTLE – COCKPIT

THE SHUTTLE CAPTAIN MAKES CONTACT WITH THE DEATH STAR.

SHUTTLE CAPTAIN

Command station, this is ST Three-twenty-one. Code Clearance Blue. We're starting our approach. Deactivate the security shield.

INTERIOR DEATH STAR CONTROL ROOM

DEATH STAR CONTROLLER

The security deflector shield will be deactivated when we have confirmation of your code transmission. Stand by. You are clear to proceed.

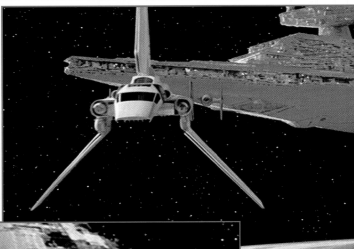

INTERIOR IMPERIAL SHUTTLE – COCKPIT

SHUTTLE CAPTAIN

We're starting our approach.

EXTERIOR SPACE

The shuttle and its two escorting TIE fighters approach, and the shuttle enters the Death Star.

INTERIOR DEATH STAR CONTROL ROOM

Operators move about among the control panels.

A control officer addresses a shield operator.

OFFICER

Inform the commander that Lord Vader's shuttle has arrived.

OPERATOR

Yes, sir.

The Imperial shuttle has landed in the massive docking bay. A squad of Imperial stormtroopers moves into formation before the craft.

INTERIOR DEATH STAR – MAIN DOCKING BAY

The Death Star Commander, Moff Jerjerrod, a tall, confident technocrat, strides through the assembled troops to the base of the shuttle ramp. The troops stand to attention; many are uneasy about the new arrival. Even the arrogant Death Star Commander swallows nervously.

THE EXIT HATCH OF THE SHUTTLE OPENS WITH A WHOOSH, REVEALING ONLY DARKNESS. THEN, HEAVY FOOTSTEPS AND MECHANICAL BREATHING. FROM THIS BLACK VOID APPEARS DARTH VADER, LORD OF THE SITH. VADER LOOKS OVER THE ASSEMBLAGE AS HE WALKS DOWN THE RAMP.

JERJERROD
_____

Lord Vader, this is an unexpected pleasure. We're honored by your presence.

VADER
_____

You may dispense with the pleasantries, Commander I'm here to put you back on schedule.

THE COMMANDER TURNS ASHEN AND BEGINS TO TREMBLE.

JERJERROD
_____

I assure you, Lord Vader, my men are working as fast as they can.

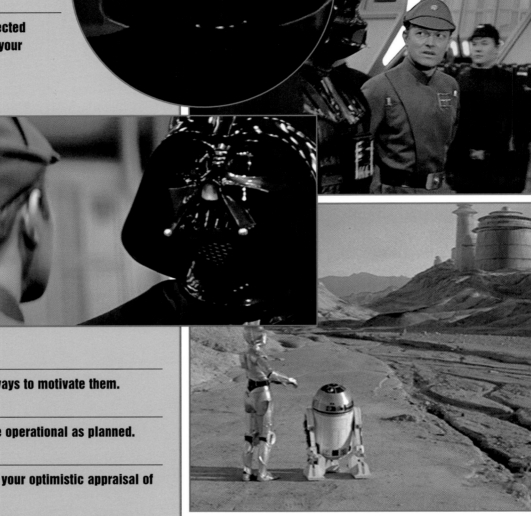

VADER
_____

Perhaps I can find new ways to motivate them.

JERJERROD
_____

I tell you, this station will be operational as planned.

VADER
_____

The Emperor does not share your optimistic appraisal of the situation.

JERJERROD
_____

But he asks the impossible. I need more men.

VADER
_____

Then perhaps you can tell him when he arrives.

JERJERROD (AGHAST)
_____

The Emperor's coming here?

VADER
_____

That is correct, Commander. And he is most displeased with your apparent lack of progress.

JERJERROD
_____

We shall double our efforts.

VADER
_____

I hope so, Commander, for your sake. The Emperor is not as forgiving as I am.

EXTERIOR ROAD TO JABBA'S PALACE – TATOOINE

A LONELY, WINDSWEPT ROAD MEANDERS THROUGH THE DESOLATE TATOOINE TERRAIN. ARTOO-DETOO AND SEE-THREEPIO ARE MAKING THEIR WAY ALONG THE ROAD TOWARD THE OMINOUS PALACE OF JABBA THE HUTT. ARTOO BEEPS.

THREEPIO
_____

Of course I'm worried. And you should be, too. Lando Calrissian and poor Chewbacca never returned from this awful place.

ARTOO WHISTLES TIMIDLY.

THREEPIO
_____

Don't be so sure. If I told you half the things I've heard about this Jabba the Hutt, you'd probably short-circuit.

THE TWO DROIDS FEARFULLY APPROACH THE MASSIVE GATE TO THE PALACE.

EXTERIOR JABBA'S PALACE – GATE

THREEPIO

Artoo, are you sure this is the right place?

THREEPIO LOOKS AROUND FOR SOME KIND OF SIGNALING DEVICE.

THREEPIO

I'd better knock, I suppose.

HE TIMIDLY KNOCKS ON THE IRON DOOR.

THREEPIO (INSTANTLY)

There doesn't seem to be anyone there. Let's go back and tell Master Luke.

A SMALL HATCH IN THE MIDDLE OF THE DOOR OPENS AND A SPIDERY MECHANICAL ARM, WITH A LARGE ELECTRONIC EYEBALL ON THE END, POPS OUT AND INSPECTS THE TWO DROIDS.

STRANGE VOICE

Tee chuta hhat yudd!

THREEPIO

Goodness gracious me!

THE EYE CONTINUES TO JABBER IN ITS STRANGE LANGUAGE. THREEPIO POINTS TO ARTOO, THEN TO HIMSELF.

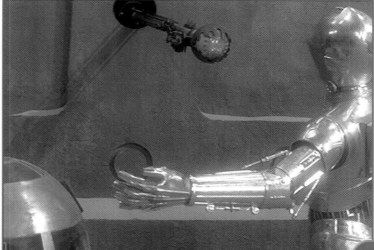

THREEPIO

Artoo Detoowha bo Seethreepiowha ey toota odd mishka Jabba du Hutt.

THE EYE POKES FORWARD TOWARDS THREEPIO, THERE IS A LAUGH, THEN THE EYE ZIPS BACK INTO THE DOOR. THE HATCH SLAMS SHUT.

THREEPIO

I don't think they're going to let us in, Artoo. We'd better go.

ARTOO BEEPS HIS RELUCTANCE AS THREEPIO TURNS TO LEAVE. SUDDENLY, THE MASSIVE DOOR STARTS TO RISE WITH A HORRIFIC METALLIC SCREECH. THE ROBOTS TURN BACK AND FACE AN ENDLESS BLACK CAVITY.

ARTOO STARTS FORWARD INTO THE GLOOM.

THREEPIO

Artoo, wait. Oh, dear! Artoo, Artoo, I really don't think we should rush into all this.

THREEPIO RUSHES AFTER HIS STUBBY COMPANION. ARTOO CONTINUES DOWN THE CORRIDOR, WITH THREEPIO FOLLOWING.

THREEPIO

Oh, Artoo! Artoo, wait for me!

INTERIOR JABBA'S PALACE – HALLWAY

The frightened robots are met by two giant, green Gamorrean guards. One guard grunts an order. Artoo beeps nervously.

THREEPIO

Just you deliver Master Luke's message and get us out of here. Oh, my!

The door slams shut with a loud crash that echoes throughout the dark passageway.

THREEPIO

Oh, no.

Walking toward them out of the darkness is Bib Fortuna, a humanlike alien with long tentacles protruding from his skull.

BIB

Die Wanna Wanga!

THREEPIO

Oh, my! Die Wanna Wauaga We – we bring a message to your master, Jabba the Hutt...

Artoo lets out a series of quick beeps.

THREEPIO (CONTINUING)

...and a gift.

(THINKS FOR A MOMENT, THEN TO ARTOO)

Gift, what gift?

BIB SHAKES HIS HEAD NEGATIVELY.

BIB

Nee Iabba no badda. Me chaade su goodie.

BIB HOLDS OUT HIS HAND TOWARDS ARTOO AND THE TINY DROID BACKS UP A BIT, LETTING OUT A PROTESTING ARRAY OF SQUEAKS. THREEPIO TURNS TO THE STRANGE-LOOKING ALIEN.

THREEPIO

He says that our instructions are to give it only to Jabba himself!

BIB THINKS ABOUT THIS FOR A MOMENT.

THREEPIO

I'm terribly sorry. I'm afraid he's ever so stubborn about these sort of things.

BIB GESTURES FOR THE DROIDS TO FOLLOW.

BIB

Nudd Chaa.

THE DROIDS FOLLOW THE TALL, TENTACLED ALIEN INTO THE DARKNESS, TRAILED BY THE TWO GUARDS.

THREEPIO

Artoo, I have a bad feeling about this.

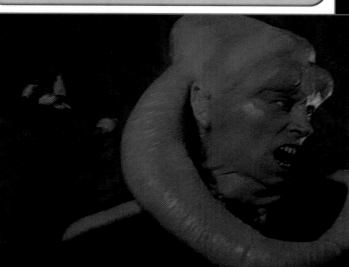

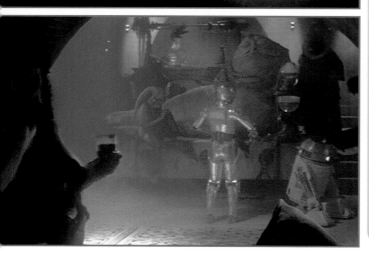

INTERIOR JABBA'S THRONE ROOM

THE THRONE ROOM IS FILLED WITH THE VILEST, MOST GROTESQUE CREATURES EVER CONCEIVED IN THE UNIVERSE. ARTOO AND THREEPIO SEEM VERY SMALL AS THEY PAUSE IN THE DOORWAY TO THE DIMLY LIT CHAMBER.

LIGHT SHAFTS PARTIALLY ILLUMINATE THE DRUNKEN COURTIERS AS BIB FORTUNA CROSSES THE ROOM TO THE PLATFORM UPON WHICH RESTS THE LEADER OF THIS NAUSEATING CROWD: JABBA THE HUTT. THE MONARCH OF THE GALACTIC UNDERWORLD IS A REPULSIVE BLOB OF BLOATED FAT WITH A MANIACAL GRIN. CHAINED TO THE HORRIBLE CREATURE IS THE BEAUTIFUL ALIEN DANCER NAMED OOLA. AT THE FOOT OF THE DAIS SITS AN OBNOXIOUS BIRDLIKE CREATURE, SALACIOUS CRUMB.

BIB WHISPERS SOMETHING IN THE SLOBBERING DEGENERATE'S EAR. JABBA LAUGHS, HORRIBLY, AT THE TWO TERRIFIED DROIDS BEFORE HIM. THREEPIO BOWS POLITELY.

THREEPIO

Good morning. The message, Artoo, the message.

JABBA

Bo Shuda!

ARTOO WHISTLES, AND A BEAM OF LIGHT PROJECTS FROM HIS DOMED HEAD, CREATING A HOLOGRAM OF LUKE ON THE FLOOR.

THE IMAGE GROWS TO OVER TEN FEET TALL, AND THE YOUNG JEDI TOWERS OVER THE SPACE GANGSTERS.

LUKE

Greetings, Exalted One. Allow me to introduce myself. I am Luke Skywalker, Jedi Knight and friend to Captain Solo. I know that you are powerful, mighty Jabba, and that your anger with Solo must be equally powerful. I seek an audience with your Greatness to bargain for Solo's life.

(JABBA'S CROWD LAUGHS)

With your wisdom, I'm sure that we can work out an arrangement which will be mutually beneficial and enable us to avoid any unpleasant confrontation. As a token of my goodwill, I present to you a gift: these two droids.

THREEPIO IS STARTLED BY THIS ANNOUNCEMENT.

THREEPIO

What did he say?

LUKE (CONTINUING)

Both are hardworking and will serve you well.

THREEPIO

This can't be! Artoo, you're playing the wrong message.

LUKE'S HOLOGRAM DISAPPEARS.

BIB SPEAKS TO JABBA IN HUTTESE.

JABBA (IN HUTTESE SUBTITLED)

There will be no bargain.

THREEPIO

We're doomed.

JABBA (IN HUTTESE SUBTITLED)

I will not give up my favorite decoration. I like Captain Solo where he is.

JABBA LOOKS TOWARD AN ALCOVE BESIDE THE THRONE. HANGING HIGH, FLAT AGAINST THE WALL, EXACTLY AS WE SAW HIM LAST, IS A CARBONIZED HAN SOLO.

THREEPIO

Artoo, look! Captain Solo. And he's still frozen in carbonite.

One of Jabba's Gamorrean guards marches Artoo and Threepio down a dank, shadowy passageway lined with holding cells. The cries of unspeakable creatures bounce off the cold stone walls. Occasionally a repulsive arm or tentacle grabs through the bars at the hapless droids.

THREEPIO

What could possibly have come over Master Luke. Is it something I did? He never expressed any unhappiness with my work. Oh! Oh! How horrid!

A large tentacle wraps around Threepio's neck.

THREEPIO

Ohh!

012

He manages to break free. Artoo beeps pitifully and they move on to a door at the end of the corridor.

INTERIOR BOILER ROOM

The door slides open, revealing a room filled with steam and noisy machinery. The guard has motioned them into the boiler room, where a power droid is upside down. As smoking brands are pressed into his feet, the stubby robot lets out an agonized electronic scream. Threepio cringes. They are met by a tall, thin humanlike robot named EV-9D9 (Eve-Ninedenine).

NINEDENINE

Ah, good. New acquisitions. You are a protocol droid, are you not?

THREEPIO

I am See-Threepio, human–cy–

NINEDENINE

Yes or no will do.

THREEPIO

Oh. Well, yes.

NINEDENINE

How many languages do you speak?

THREEPIO

I am fluent in over six million forms of communication and can readily –

NINEDENINE

Splendid! We have been without an interpreter since our master got angry with our last protocol droid and disintegrated him.

THREEPIO

Disintegrated?

NINEDENINE (TO A GAMORREAN GUARD)

Guard! This protocol droid might be useful. Fit him with a restraining bolt and take him back to His Excellency's main audience chamber.

The guard shoves Threepio toward the door.

THREEPIO (DISAPPEARING)

Artoo, don't leave me! Ohhh!

Artoo lets out a plaintive cry as the door closes. Then he beeps angrily.

NINEDENINE

You're a feisty little one, but you'll soon learn some respect. I have need for you on the master's sail barge. And I think you'll fit in nicely.

The poor work droid in the background lets out another tortured electronic scream.

The court of Jabba the Hutt is in the midst of a drunken, raucous party. Sloppy, smelly monsters cheer and make rude noises as Oola and a large six-breasted female dancer perform in front of Jabba's throne. Jabba's alien band plays a wildly rhythmic tune on reeds, drums, and other exotic instruments. The Hutt rocks and swings in time with the music and toys with Oola's leash. The song comes to a close, and the audience applauds.

JABBA

Ah! Do that again!

The band begins again.

JOH YOWZA

One, two, three!

The band starts to play the wrong song.

JOH YOWZA

No, daddy, no! One, two, three!

The music swells. Oola and the other dancer perform as the alien band rocks. Jabba leers at the dancers and with a lustful gleam in his eye beckons Oola to come and sit with him. She stops dancing and backs away, shaking her head. Jabba gets angry and pulls on her leash, pointing to a spot next to him. Oola continues to protest and pull back against the taut leash.

JABBA

Da Eitha!

The lovely alien shakes her head again and screams.

OOLA

Na Chuba negtorie Na! Na! Natoota...

Jabba is furious and pulls her toward him, tugging on the chain.

JABBA

Boscka!

Jabba slams his fist down on a button, and before the dancer can flee, a trap-door in the floor springs open and swallows her up. As the door snaps shut, a muffled growl is followed by a hideous scream.

JABBA AND HIS MONSTROUS FRIENDS LAUGH HYSTERICALLY, AND SEVERAL REVELERS HURRY OVER TO WATCH HER FATE THROUGH THE GRATE. OOLA TUMBLES DOWN A CHUTE AND SPRAWLS ON THE FLOOR OF THE RANCOR CAGE.

THREEPIO CRINGES AND GLANCES WISTFULLY AT THE CARBONITE FORM OF HAN SOLO, BUT IS DISTRACTED BY A GUNSHOT OFFSCREEN. AN UNNATURAL QUIET SWEEPS THE BOISTEROUS GATHERING.

ON THE FAR SIDE OF THE ROOM, THE CRUSH OF DEBAUCHERS MOVES ASIDE TO ALLOW THE APPROACH OF BOUSHH, AN ODDLY CLOAKED BOUNTY HUNTER, LEADING HIS CAPTIVE, HAN SOLO'S CO-PILOT, CHEWBACCA THE WOOKIEE.

THE BOUNTY HUNTER BOWS BEFORE THE GANGSTER AND SPEAKS A GREETING IN A STRANGE, ELECTRONICALLY PROCESSED TONGUE (UBESE).

BOUSHH (IN UBESE SUBTITLED)

I have come for the bounty on this Wookiee.

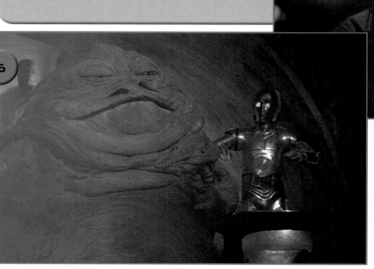

THREEPIO

Oh, no! Chewbacca!

JABBA (IN HUTTESE SUBTITLED)

At last we have the mighty Chewbacca.

JABBA CALLS FOR THREEPIO. THE RELUCTANT DROID OBEYS.

THREEPIO

Oh, uh, yes, uh, I am here, Your Worshipfulness. Uh…yes!

JABBA CONTINUES SPEAKING, AS THREEPIO NERVOUSLY TRANSLATES.

THREEPIO

Oh. The illustrious Jabba bids you welcome and will gladly pay you the reward of twenty-five thousand.

BOUSHH (IN UBESE SUBTITLED)

I want fifty thousand. No less.

THREEPIO

Fifty thousand. No less.

JABBA IMMEDIATELY FLIES INTO A RAGE, KNOCKING THE GOLDEN DROID OFF THE RAISED THRONE INTO A CLATTERING HEAP ON THE FLOOR.

BOUSHH ADJUSTS HIS WEAPON AS JABBA RAVES IN HUTTESE AND THREEPIO STRUGGLES BACK ONTO THE THRONE. THE DISHEVELED DROID TRIES TO COMPOSE HIMSELF.

THREEPIO

Oh, oh…but what, what did I say?

(TO BOUSHH)

Uh, the mighty Jabba asks why he must pay fifty thousand.

THE BOUNTY HUNTER HOLDS UP A SMALL SILVER BALL IN HIS HAND.

THREEPIO

Because he's holding a thermal detonator.

THREEPIO IS VERY NERVOUS. THE
GUARDS INSTANTLY BACK AWAY, AS
DO MOST OF THE OTHER MONSTERS
IN THE ROOM. BUT BOBA FETT
RAISES HIS GUN. THE ROOM HAS
FALLEN INTO A TENSE HUSH. JABBA
BEGINS TO LAUGH.

JABBA (IN HUTTESE SUBTITLED)

**This bounty hunter is my kind of scum,
fearless and inventive.**

JABBA CONTINUES.

THREEPIO

**Jabba offers the sum of thirty-five. And I do
suggest you take it.**

BIB AND THE OTHER MONSTERS
STUDY THE BOUNTY HUNTER AND
WAIT FOR HIS REACTION.

BOUSHH

Zeebuss.

BOUSHH RELEASES A SWITCH ON
THE THERMAL DETONATOR AND IT
GOES DEAD.

THREEPIO

He agrees!

THE RAUCOUS CROWD OF
MONSTERS ERUPTS IN A SYMPHONY
OF CHEERS AND APPLAUSE AS THE
PARTY RETURNS TO ITS FULL NOISY
PITCH. CHEWBACCA GROWLS AND IS
LED AWAY. THE BAND STARTS UP AND
DANCING GIRLS TAKE THE CENTER OF
THE FLOOR, TO THE HOOTS OF THE
LOUDLY APPRECIATIVE CREATURES.

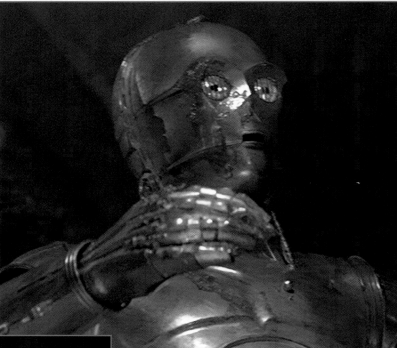

BOUSHH LEANS AGAINST A COLUMN WITH GUNFIGHTER COOL AND SURVEYS THE SCENE, HIS GAZE STOPPING ONLY WHEN IT CONNECTS WITH A GLARE FROM ACROSS THE ROOM: BOBA FETT IS WATCHING HIM.

INTERIOR DUNGEON CORRIDOR AND CELL

GAMORREAN GUARDS LEAD CHEWIE DOWN THE SAME HALLWAY WE SAW BEFORE. AS HE IS LED AWAY WE SPOT LANDO CALRISSIAN, DISGUISED AS A SKIFF GUARD IN A PARTIAL FACE MASK. WHEN A TENTACLE REACHES OUT AT THE WOOKIEE, CHEWIE'S FEROCIOUS ROAR ECHOES AGAINST THE WALLS AND THE TENTACLE SNAPS BACK INTO ITS CELL IN TERROR. IT TAKES BOTH THE GUARDS TO HURL CHEWIE ROUGHLY INTO A CELL, SLAMMING THE DOOR BEHIND HIM.

EXTERIOR JABBA'S PALACE

THE PALACE IS SITTING IN THE LIGHT OF THE DOUBLE SUNSET. ON THE ROAD IN FRONT, A LARGE TOADLIKE CREATURE FLICKS ITS TONGUE OUT FOR A DESERT RODENT, AND BURPS IN SATISFACTION.

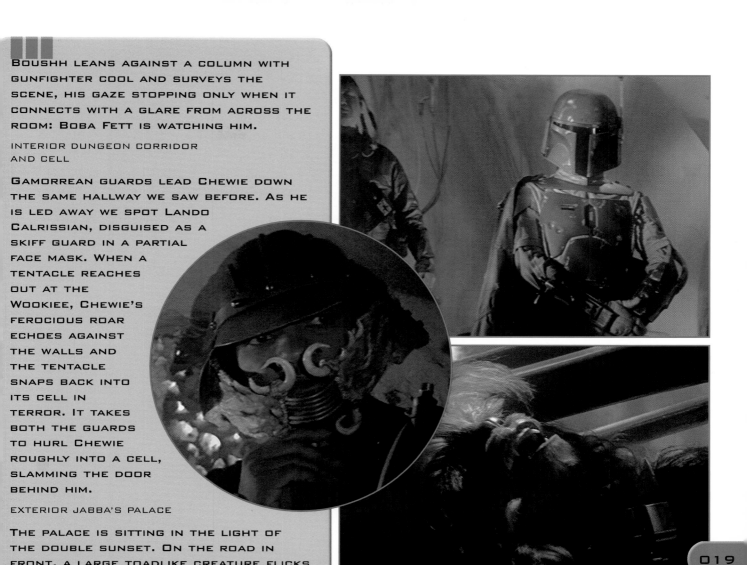

JABBA'S THRONE ROOM – NIGHT

SILENCE. THE ROOM IS DESERTED, ONLY THE AWFUL DEBRIS OF THE ALIEN CELEBRATION GIVING MUTE WITNESS TO THE ACTIVITY HERE BEFORE. SEVERAL DRUNK CREATURES LIE UNCONSCIOUS AROUND THE ROOM, SNORING LOUDLY.

A SHADOWY FIGURE MOVES STEALTHILY AMONG THE COLUMNS AT THE PERIMETER OF THE ROOM AND IS REVEALED TO BE BOUSHH, THE BOUNTY HUNTER. HE PICKS HIS WAY CAREFULLY THROUGH THE SNORING, DRUNKEN MONSTERS.

HAN SOLO, THE FROZEN SPACE PIRATE, HANGS SPOTLIGHTED ON THE WALL, HIS COFFINLIKE CASE SUSPENDED BY A FORCE FIELD. THE BOUNTY HUNTER DEACTIVATES THE FORCE FIELD BY FLIPPING A CONTROL SWITCH TO ONE SIDE OF THE COFFIN.

THE HEAVY CASE SLOWLY LOWERS TO THE FLOOR OF THE ALCOVE.

020

BOUSHH STEPS UP TO THE CASE, STUDYING HAN, THEN TURNS TO THE CONTROLS ON THE SIDE OF THE COFFIN. HE ACTIVATES A SERIES OF SWITCHES AND SLIDES THE DECARBONIZATION LEVER. THE CASE BEGINS TO EMIT A SOUND AS THE HARD SHELL COVERING THE CONTOURS OF HAN'S FACE BEGINS TO MELT AWAY. THE BOUNTY HUNTER WATCHES AS HAN'S BODY IS FREED OF ITS METALLIC COAT AND HIS FOREARMS AND HANDS, PREVIOUSLY RAISED IN REFLEXIVE PROTEST, DROP SLACKLY TO HIS SIDE. HIS FACE MUSCLES RELAX FROM THEIR MASK OF HORROR. HE APPEARS QUITE DEAD.

BOUSHH'S UGLY HELMET LEANS CLOSE TO HAN'S FACE LISTENING FOR THE BREATH OF LIFE. NOTHING. HE WAITS. HAN'S EYES POP OPEN WITH A START AND HE BEGINS SHAKING. THE BOUNTY HUNTER STEADIES THE STAGGERING NEWBORN.

BOUSHH

Just relax for a moment. You're free of the carbonite.

HAN TOUCHES HIS FACE WITH HIS HAND.

BOUSHH

Shh. You have hibernation sickness.

HAN

I can't see.

BOUSHH

Your eyesight will return in time.

HAN

Where am I?

BOUSHH

Jabba's palace.

HAN

Who are you?

THE BOUNTY HUNTER REACHES UP AND LIFTS THE HELMET FROM HIS HEAD, REVEALING THE BEAUTIFUL FACE OF PRINCESS LEIA.

LEIA

Someone who loves you.

HAN

Leia!

LEIA

I gotta get you out of here.

AS LEIA HELPS HER WEAKENED LOVER TO
STAND UP, THE RELATIVE QUIET IS PIERCED
BY AN OBSCENE HUTTESE CACKLE FROM THE
OTHER SIDE OF THE ALCOVE.

HAN

What's that? I know that laugh.

THE CURTAIN ON THE FAR SIDE OF THE
ALCOVE OPENS, REVEALING JABBA THE
HUTT, SURROUNDED BY BIB AND OTHER
ALIENS. HE LAUGHS AGAIN, AND HIS
GROSS CRONIES JOIN IN A CACOPHONY
OF ALIEN GLEE.

HAN

Hey, Jabba. Look, Jabba. I was just on my way
to pay you back but I got a little sidetracked. It's
not my fault.

JABBA LAUGHS.

JABBA (IN HUTTESE SUBTITLED)

It's too late for that, Solo. You may have been
a good smuggler, but now you're bantha
fodder.

HAN

Look –

**JABBA (CONTINUING;
IN HUTTESE SUBTITLED)**

Take him away!

THE GUARDS GRAB HAN AND START TO LEAD HIM AWAY.

HAN

Jabba...I'll pay you triple! You're throwing away a fortune here. Don't be a fool!

HAN IS DRAGGED OFF.

JABBA (IN HUTTESE SUBTITLED)

Bring her to me.

JABBA CHUCKLES AS LANDO AND A SECOND GUARD LEAD THE BEAUTIFUL YOUNG PRINCESS TOWARD HIM.

LEIA

We have powerful friends. You're gonna regret this.

JABBA (IN HUTTESE SUBTITLED)

I'm sure.

INEXORABLY HER LOVELY FACE MOVES TO WITHIN A FEW INCHES OF JABBA'S UGLY BLOB OF A HEAD.

LEIA (TURNING AWAY IN DISGUST)

Ugh!

THREEPIO

Ohhh!

(QUICKLY TURNING AWAY IN DISGUST)

I can't bear to watch.

INTERIOR DUNGEON CELL

THE BLINDED STAR CAPTAIN IS THROWN
INTO THE DUNGEON AND THE DOOR SLAMS
BEHIND HIM, LEAVING ONLY A THIN SLIVER
OF LIGHT FROM A CRACK IN THE CEILING.
HAN IS TRYING TO COLLECT HIMSELF WHEN
SUDDENLY A GROWL IS HEARD FROM THE
FAR SIDE OF THE CELL. HE LISTENS.

HAN

Chewie? Chewie, is that you?

THE SHADOWY FIGURE OF
CHEWIE LETS OUT A CRAZY
YELL AND RACES TOWARD HAN,
HUGGING HIM.

HAN

Chew – Chewie!

THE GIANT WOOKIEE BARKS
WITH GLEE.

HAN

Wait, I can't see, pal. What's goin' on?

CHEWIE BARKS AN EXCITED
BLUE STREAK.

HAN

Luke? Luke's crazy. He can't even take
care of himself, much less rescue
anybody.

CHEWIE BARKS A REPLY.

HAN

A – a Jedi Knight? I'm out of it for a little while,
everybody gets delusions of grandeur.

CHEWIE GROWLS INSISTENTLY. HE HOLDS
HAN TO HIS CHEST AND PETS HIS HEAD.

HAN

I'm all right, pal. I'm all right.

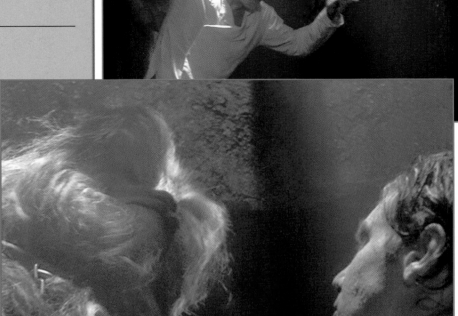

INTERIOR MAIN GATE AND HALL – JABBA'S PALACE

NOISILY, THE MAIN GATE LIFTS TO FLOOD
THE BLACKNESS WITH BLINDING LIGHT AND
REVEAL THE SILHOUETTED FIGURE OF LUKE
SKYWALKER. HE IS CLAD IN A ROBE SIMILAR
TO BEN'S AND WEARS NEITHER PISTOL NOR
LASER SWORD. LUKE STRIDES
PURPOSEFULLY INTO THE HALLWAY. TWO
GIANT GUARDS MOVE TO BLOCK LUKE'S
PATH. LUKE HALTS.

LUKE RAISES HIS HAND AND POINTS AT THE
PUZZLED GUARDS, WHO IMMEDIATELY LOWER
THEIR SPEARS AND FALL BACK. THE YOUNG
JEDI LOWERS HIS HAND AND MOVES ON
DOWN THE HALLWAY.

INTERIOR JABBA'S THRONE ROOM

JABBA IS ASLEEP ON HIS THRONE, WITH LEIA
LYING IN FRONT OF HIM. SALACIOUS SITS BY
JABBA'S TAIL, WATCHING IT WRIGGLE. LEIA IS
NOW DRESSED IN THE SKIMPY COSTUME OF A
DANCING GIRL; A CHAIN RUNS FROM A
MANACLE/NECKLACE AT HER THROAT TO HER
NEW MASTER, JABBA THE HUTT. THREEPIO
STANDS BEHIND JABBA.

BIB FORTUNA APPEARS OUT OF THE GLOOM.
HE SPEAKS TO LUKE AS THEY APPROACH
EACH OTHER.

LUKE

I must speak with Jabba.

BIB ANSWERS IN HUTTESE, SHAKING HIS HEAD
IN DENIAL.

INTERIOR JABBA'S THRONE ROOM

LEIA LOOKS UP IN RECOGNITION OF LUKE'S
VOICE.

INTERIOR MAIN GATE AND HALL – JABBA'S PALACE

LUKE STOPS AND STARES AT BIB; HE RAISES
HIS HAND SLIGHTLY.

LUKE

You will take me to Jabba now!

BIB TURNS IN HYPNOTIC RESPONSE TO LUKE'S
COMMAND, AND LUKE FOLLOWS HIM INTO THE
GLOOM.

LUKE

You serve your master well.

BIB RESPONDS.

LUKE

And you will be rewarded.

INTERIOR JABBA'S THRONE ROOM

BIB COMES UP TO THE GANGSTER SLUG.

THREEPIO

At last! Master Luke's come to rescue me!

BIB

Master.

JABBA AWAKENS WITH A START AND BIB
CONTINUES, IN HUTTESE.

BIB

Luke Skywalker, Jedi Knight.

JABBA (IN HUTTESE SUBTITLED)

I told you not to admit him.

LUKE

I must be allowed to speak.

BIB (IN HUTTESE SUBTITLED)

He must be allowed to speak.

JABBA, FURIOUS, SHOVES BIB AWAY. LUKE
STARES HARD AT JABBA.

JABBA (IN HUTTESE SUBTITLED)

You weak-minded fool!

(TURNING)

He's using an old Jedi mind trick.

LUKE

You will bring Captain Solo and the Wookiee to me.

JABBA (LAUGHING)
(IN HUTTESE SUBTITLED)

Your mind powers will not work on me, boy.

LUKE

Nevertheless, I'm taking Captain Solo and his friends. You can either profit by this…or be destroyed! It's your choice. But I warn you not to underestimate my powers.

JABBA SMILES. THREEPIO ATTEMPTS TO WARN LUKE ABOUT THE PIT.

THREEPIO

Master Luke, you're standing on…

JABBA (IN HUTTESE SUBTITLED)

There will be no bargain, young Jedi. I shall enjoy watching you die.

LUKE REACHES OUT, AND A PISTOL JUMPS OUT OF A GUARD'S HOLSTER AND FLIES INTO LUKE'S HAND. THE BEWILDERED GUARD GRABS FOR IT AS JABBA RAISES HIS HAND.

JABBA

Boscka!

THE FLOOR SUDDENLY DROPS AWAY, SENDING LUKE AND THE HAPLESS GUARD INTO THE PIT. THE PISTOL GOES OFF, BLASTING A HOLE IN THE CEILING.

INTERIOR RANCOR PIT

LUKE AND THE GUARD HAVE DROPPED TWENTY-FIVE FEET FROM A CHUTE INTO THE DUNGEONLIKE CAGE. LUKE GETS TO HIS FEET AS THE GUARD YELLS HYSTERICALLY FOR HELP.

INTERIOR JABBA'S THRONE ROOM

JABBA LAUGHS AND HIS COURTIERS JOIN HIM. LEIA STARTS FORWARD BUT IS COMFORTED BY A HUMAN GUARD – LANDO, RECOGNIZABLE BEHIND HIS MASK.

INTERIOR RANCOR PIT

A CROWD HAS GATHERED UP AROUND THE EDGE OF THE PIT AS A DOOR IN THE SIDE OF THE PIT STARTS TO RUMBLE OPEN.

THREEPIO

Oh, no! The rancor!

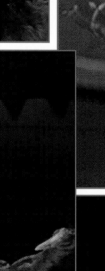

027

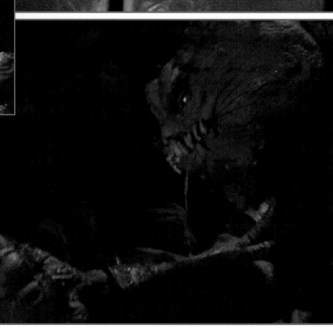

AT THE SIDE OF THE PIT, AN IRON DOOR RUMBLES UPWARD AND A GIANT, FANGED RANCOR EMERGES. THE GUARD RUNS TO THE SIDE OF THE PIT AND TRIES FUTILELY TO SCRAMBLE TO THE TOP. THE HIDEOUS BEAST CLOSES IN ON HIM.

INTERIOR JABBA'S THRONE ROOM

THE SPECTATORS LOOK ON.

INTERIOR RANCOR PIT

THE RANCOR MOVES PAST LUKE, AND AS THE GUARD CONTINUES TO SCRAMBLE, THE RANCOR PICKS HIM UP AND POPS HIM INTO ITS SLAVERING JAWS. A FEW SCREAMS, AND THE GUARD IS SWALLOWED WITH A GULP.

INTERIOR JABBA'S THRONE ROOM

THE AUDIENCE CHEERS AND LAUGHS AT THE GUARD'S FATE.

INTERIOR RANCOR PIT

THE MONSTER TURNS AND STARTS FOR LUKE.

INTERIOR JABBA'S THRONE ROOM

JABBA SMILES.

INTERIOR RANCOR PIT

THE YOUNG JEDI DASHES AWAY JUST AHEAD OF THE MONSTER'S SWIPE AT HIM, AND PICKS UP THE LONG ARM BONE OF AN EARLIER VICTIM. THE MONSTER GRABS LUKE.

INTERIOR JABBA'S THRONE ROOM

THE AUDIENCE CHEERS.

INTERIOR RANCOR PIT

THE MONSTER BRINGS HIM UP TO HIS SALIVATING MOUTH.

INTERIOR JABBA'S THRONE ROOM

LEIA CAN HARDLY BEAR TO WATCH.

INTERIOR RANCOR PIT

AT THE LAST MOMENT, LUKE WEDGES THE BONE IN THE MONSTER'S MOUTH AND IS DROPPED TO THE FLOOR. THE MONSTER BELLOWS IN RAGE AND FLAILS ABOUT.

THE MONSTER CRUNCHES THE BONE IN ITS JAWS AND SEES LUKE, WHO SQUEEZES INTO A CREVICE IN THE PIT WALL. LUKE LOOKS PAST THE MONSTER TO THE HOLDING CAVE BEYOND. ON THE FAR SIDE OF THE HOLDING CAVE IS A UTILITY DOOR – IF ONLY HE CAN GET TO IT. THE RANCOR SPOTS LUKE AND REACHES INTO THE CREVICE FOR HIM. LUKE GRABS A LARGE ROCK AND RAISES IT, SMASHING IT DOWN ON THE RANCOR'S FINGER.

INTERIOR HOLDING TUNNEL – RANCOR PIT

THE RANCOR LETS OUT A HOWL AS LUKE MAKES A RUN FOR THE HOLDING CAVE. HE REACHES THE DOOR AND PUSHES A BUTTON TO OPEN IT. WHEN HE SUCCEEDS, HE SEES A HEAVY BARRED GATE BETWEEN HIM AND SAFETY. BEYOND THE GATE TWO GUARDS HAVE LOOKED UP FROM THEIR DINNER. LUKE TURNS TO SEE THE MONSTER HEADING FOR HIM, AND PULLS WITH ALL HIS MIGHT ON THE GATE. THE GUARDS MOVE TO THE GATE AND START POKING AT THE YOUNG JEDI WITH SPEARS, LAUGHING.

INTERIOR JABBA'S THRONE ROOM

THE AUDIENCE IS MAD WITH EXCITEMENT.

INTERIOR HOLDING TUNNEL – RANCOR PIT

LUKE CROUCHES (AGAINST THE WALL) AS THE MONSTER STARTS TO REACH FOR HIM. SUDDENLY HE NOTICES A MAIN DOOR CONTROL PANEL HALFWAY UP THE WALL. AS THE RANCOR MOVES IN FOR THE KILL, LUKE PICKS UP A SKULL FROM THE CAVE FLOOR AND HURLS IT AT THE PANEL. A SPLIT SECOND BEFORE THE RANCOR REACHES LUKE, THE PANEL EXPLODES.

THE GIANT OVERHEAD DOOR COMES
CRASHING DOWN ON THE BEAST'S HEAD,
SQUASHING IT.

INTERIOR THRONE ROOM

A STARTLED GASP IS HEARD FROM THE
STUNNED COURT. THERE'S CONSTERNATION
AT THIS TURN OF EVENTS. HEADS LOOK TO
JABBA, WHO IS ACTUALLY TURNING RED
WITH ANGER.

INTERIOR HOLDING TUNNEL – RANCOR PIT

THE BEAST BREATHES ITS LAST.

INTERIOR THRONE ROOM

LEIA CANNOT SUPPRESS HER JOY.

INTERIOR RANCOR PIT

THE RANCOR KEEPERS HAVE COME INTO THE
CAGE AND ARE EXAMINING THEIR DEAD BEAST.
ONE OF THEM BREAKS DOWN AND WEEPS. THE
OTHER GLARES MENACINGLY AT LUKE, WHO IS
UNWORRIED. SEVERAL GUARDS RUSH INTO THE
HOLDING TUNNEL AND TAKE LUKE AWAY.

INTERIOR THRONE ROOM

JABBA UTTERS HARSH COMMANDS TO HIS
GUARDS AND THEY HURRY OFF.

JABBA (IN HUTTESE SUBTITLED)

**Bring me Solo and the Wookiee. They will all suffer for
this outrage.**

INTERIOR RANCOR PIT

THE WEEPING RANCOR KEEPER IS
CONSOLED AND LED AWAY.

INTERIOR THRONE ROOM

THE CROWD OF CREEPY COURTIERS PARTS AS
HAN AND CHEWIE ARE BROUGHT INTO THE
THRONE ROOM, AND OTHER GUARDS,
INCLUDING LANDO, DRAG LUKE UP THE STEPS.

LUKE

Han!

HAN

Luke!

LUKE

Are you all right?

HAN

Fine. Together again, huh?

LUKE

Wouldn't miss it.

HAN

How are we doing?

LUKE

The same as always.

HAN

That bad, huh? Where's Leia?

LEIA

I'm here.

THREEPIO IS STANDING
BEHIND THE GROTESQUE
GANGSTER AS HE STROKES
LEIA LIKE A PET CAT.

THREEPIO STEPS FORWARD
AND TRANSLATES FOR THE
CAPTIVES.

THREEPIO

Oh, dear. His High Exaltedness, the
great Jabba the Hutt, has decreed
that you are to be
terminated
immediately.

HAN

Good. I hate long
waits.

THREEPIO

You will therefore be
taken to the Dune Sea
and cast into the Pit of
Carkoon, the nesting
place of the
all-powerful Sarlacc.

HAN (TO LUKE)

Doesn't sound so bad.

THREEPIO

In his belly, you will
find a new definition
of pain and suffering,
as you are slowly
digested over a
thousand years.

CHEWIE BARKS.

HAN

On second thought, let's pass on that, huh?

LUKE

You should have bargained, Jabba. That's the last
mistake you'll ever make.

JABBA CACKLES EVILLY AT THIS.

AS THE GUARDS DRAG THE PRISONERS
FROM THE THRONE ROOM, LEIA LOOKS
CONCERNED, BUT LUKE SKYWALKER, JEDI
WARRIOR, CANNOT SUPPRESS A SMILE.

EXTERIOR TATOOINE DUNE SEA

A HERD OF WILD BANTHAS TREK ACROSS
TATOOINE'S DUNES.

EXTERIOR TATOOINE DUNE SEA

JABBA'S HUGE SAIL BARGE MOVES ABOVE
THE DESERT SURFACE ACCOMPANIED BY TWO
SMALLER SKIFFS.

INTERIOR BARGE OBSERVATION DECK

JABBA'S ENTIRE RETINUE IS TRAVELING WITH
HIM, DRINKING, EATING, AND HAVING A GOOD
TIME.

EXTERIOR TATOOINE DUNE SEA

THE SAIL BARGE AND SKIFFS CONTINUE
THEIR JOURNEY.

INTERIOR BARGE OBSERVATION DECK

JABBA THE HUTT RIDES LIKE A SULTAN IN THE
MASSIVE ANTIGRAVITY SHIP. LEIA IS WATCHING
HER FRIENDS IN ONE OF THE SKIFFS.

EXTERIOR TATOOINE DUNE SEA – SKIFF

THE SKIFF GLIDES CLOSE, REVEALING LUKE,
HAN, AND CHEWIE – ALL IN BONDS –
SURROUNDED BY GUARDS, ONE OF WHOM IS
LANDO IN DISGUISE.

HAN

I think my eyes are getting better. Instead of a big dark
blur, I see a big light blur.

LUKE

There's nothing to see. I used to live here, you know.

HAN

You're gonna die here, you know. Convenient.

LUKE

Just stick close to Chewie and Lando. I've taken care
of everything.

HAN

Oh…great!

INTERIOR BARGE OBSERVATION DECK

THE CHAIN ATTACHED TO LEIA'S NECK IS
PULLED TIGHT, AND JABBA TUGS THE
SCANTILY CLAD PRINCESS TO HIM.

JABBA (IN HUTTESE SUBTITLED)

Soon you will learn to appreciate me.

THREEPIO WANDERS AMONG THE SAIL BARGE
ALIENS, BUMPING INTO A SMALLER DROID
SERVING DRINKS, SPILLING THEM ALL OVER
THE PLACE. THE STUBBY DROID LETS OUT
AN ANGRY SERIES OF BEEPS AND WHISTLES.

THREEPIO

Oh, I'm terribly sor...Artoo! What are you doing here?

ARTOO BEEPS A QUICK REPLY.

THREEPIO

Well, I can see you're serving drinks, but this place is dangerous. They're going to execute Master Luke and, if we're not careful, us too!

ARTOO WHISTLES A SINGSONG RESPONSE.

THREEPIO

Hmm. I wish I had your confidence.

EXTERIOR SARLACC PIT

THE CONVOY MOVES UP OVER A HUGE SAND PIT. THE SAIL BARGE STOPS TO ONE SIDE OF THE DEPRESSION, AS DOES THE ESCORT SKIFF. BUT THE PRISONERS' SKIFF MOVES OUT DIRECTLY OVER THE CENTER AND HOVERS. A PLANK IS EXTENDED FROM THE EDGE OF THE PRISONERS' SKIFF. AT THE BOTTOM OF THE DEEP CONE OF SAND IS A REPULSIVE, MUCOUS-LINED HOLE, SURROUNDED BY THOUSANDS OF NEEDLE-SHARP TEETH. THIS IS THE SARLACC. GUARDS RELEASE LUKE'S BONDS AND SHOVE HIM OUT ON TO THE PLANK ABOVE THE SARLACC'S MOUTH.

INTERIOR SAIL BARGE OBSERVATION DECK

JABBA AND LEIA ARE NOW BY THE RAIL, WATCHING.

EXTERIOR SAIL BARGE

THREEPIO'S VOICE IS AMPLIFIED ACROSS LOUDSPEAKERS.

THREEPIO

Victims of the almighty Sarlacc: His Excellency hopes that you will die honorably. But should any of you wish to beg for mercy...

INTERIOR SAIL BARGE OBSERVATION DECK

BIB LISTENS GLEEFULLY.

EXTERIOR SAIL BARGE

THREEPIO

...the great Jabba the Hutt will now listen to your pleas.

INTERIOR SAIL BARGE OBSERVATION DECK

JABBA WAITS AS ARTOO ZIPS UNNOTICED UP THE RAMP TO THE UPPER DECK.

EXTERIOR SKIFF

HAN STEPS FORWARD ARROGANTLY AND BEGINS TO SPEAK.

HAN

Threepio, you tell that slimy piece of worm-ridden filth he'll get no such pleasure from us. Right?

CHEWIE GROWLS HIS AGREEMENT. ARTOO APPEARS ON THE UPPER DECK OF THE SAIL BARGE.

LUKE

Jabba! This is your last chance. Free us or die.

INTERIOR SAIL BARGE
OBSERVATION DECK

THE ASSEMBLED MONSTERS ROCK
WITH MOCKING LAUGHTER.
JABBA'S LAUGHTER SUBSIDES AS
HE SPEAKS INTO THE COMLINK.

JABBA (IN HUTTESE SUBTITLED)

Move him into position.

EXTERIOR SKIFF – PLANK

LUKE IS PRODDED BY A
GUARD TO THE EDGE OF THE
PLANK OVER THE GAPING
SARLACC! HE EXCHANGES
NODS WITH LANDO.

EXTERIOR BARGE – UPPER DECK

ARTOO IS AT THE RAIL
FACING THE PIT.

EXTERIOR SKIFF – PLANK

HAN LOOKS AROUND FOR A
WAY OUT OF THEIR PLIGHT.

INTERIOR SAIL BARGE
   OBSERVATION DECK

LEIA LOOKS WORRIED.

EXTERIOR SKIFF – PLANK

LUKE LOOKS UP AT
ARTOO, THEN GIVES A
JAUNTY SALUTE: THE SIGNAL
THE LITTLE DROID HAS BEEN
WAITING FOR.

EXTERIOR BARGE – UPPER DECK

A FLAP OPENS IN ARTOO'S DOMED HEAD.

INTERIOR SAIL BARGE OBSERVATION DECK

JABBA (IN HUTTESE SUBTITLED)

Put him in.

EXTERIOR SKIFF – PLANK

LUKE IS PRODDED AND JUMPS OFF THE
PLANK TO THE CHEERS OF THE
BLOODTHIRSTY SPECTATORS. BUT, BEFORE
ANYONE CAN EVEN PERCEIVE WHAT IS
HAPPENING, HE SPINS AROUND AND GRABS
THE END OF THE PLANK BY HIS FINGERTIPS.
THE PLANK BENDS WILDLY FROM HIS WEIGHT
AND CATAPULTS HIM SKYWARD.

EXTERIOR BARGE – UPPER DECK

ARTOO SENDS LUKE'S LIGHT SABER ARCING
TOWARD HIM.

EXTERIOR SKIFF

IN MIDAIR HE DOES A COMPLETE FLIP AND
DROPS DOWN INTO THE SKIFF. HE CASUALLY
EXTENDS AN OPEN PALM — AND HIS
LIGHTSABER DROPS INTO HIS HAND.

WITH SAMURAI SPEED, LUKE IGNITES IT AND
ATTACKS THE GUARDS. THE OTHER GUARDS
SWARM TOWARD LUKE. HE WADES INTO
THEM, LIGHTSABER FLASHING.

EXTERIOR SARLACC PIT

A GUARD FALLS OVERBOARD AND LANDS IN
THE SOFT, SANDY SLOPE OF THE PIT, AND
BEGINS SLIDING INTO THE PIT.

INTERIOR SAIL BARGE

JABBA WATCHES THIS AND EXPLODES IN
RAGE. HE BARKS COMMANDS, AND THE
GUARDS AROUND HIM RUSH OFF TO DO HIS
BIDDING. THE SCUZZY CREATURES WATCHING
THE ACTION FROM THE WINDOW ARE IN AN
UPROAR.

EXTERIOR SKIFF

LUKE KNOCKS ANOTHER GUARD OFF
THE SKIFF AND INTO THE WAITING
MOUTH OF THE SARLACC. HE STARTS
TO UNTIE CHEWIE'S BONDS.

LUKE

Easy, Chewie.

EXTERIOR UPPER DECK — SAIL BARGE

THE DECK GUNMEN ON THE BARGE SET
UP A CANNON ON THE UPPER DECK.

EXTERIOR SKIFF

LANDO STRUGGLES WITH A GUARD AT
THE BACK OF THE SKIFF.

AT THAT MOMENT, A DECK GUNMAN UNLEASHES A BLAST FROM HIS CANNON.

EXTERIOR SKIFF

LANDO IS TOSSED FROM THE DECK OF THE ROCKING SKIFF. HE MANAGES TO GRAB A ROPE AND DANGLES DESPERATELY ABOVE THE SARLACC PIT.

LANDO

Whoa! Whoa! Help!

EXTERIOR UPPER DECK – SAIL BARGE

WITH TWO SWIFT STRIDES, THE DANGEROUS BOBA FETT IGNITES HIS ROCKET PACK, LEAPS INTO THE AIR, AND FLIES FROM THE BARGE DOWN TO THE SKIFF.

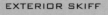

EXTERIOR SKIFF

BOBA LANDS ON THE SKIFF AND STARTS TO AIM HIS LASER GUN AT LUKE, WHO HAS FREED HAN AND CHEWIE FROM THEIR BONDS. BUT BEFORE BOBA CAN FIRE, THE YOUNG JEDI SPINS ON HIM, LIGHTSABER SWEEPING, AND HACKS THE BOUNTY HUNTER'S GUN IN HALF.

IMMEDIATELY, THE SKIFF TAKES ANOTHER DIRECT HIT FROM THE BARGE'S DECK GUN. SHARDS OF SKIFF DECK FLY. CHEWIE AND HAN ARE THROWN AGAINST THE RAIL.

HAN

Chewie, you okay? Where is he?

THE WOOKIEE IS WOUNDED AND HE HOWLS IN PAIN.

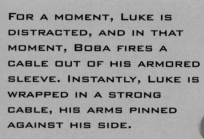

FOR A MOMENT, LUKE IS DISTRACTED, AND IN THAT MOMENT, BOBA FIRES A CABLE OUT OF HIS ARMORED SLEEVE. INSTANTLY, LUKE IS WRAPPED IN A STRONG CABLE, HIS ARMS PINNED AGAINST HIS SIDE.

EXTERIOR UPPER DECK – SAIL BARGE

THE DECK GUNMAN CONTINUES TO BLAST THE SKIFF WITH HIS CANNON.

EXTERIOR SKIFF

LUKE'S SWORD ARM IS FREE ONLY FROM THE WRIST DOWN. HE BENDS HIS WRIST SO THE LIGHTSABER POINTS STRAIGHT UP TO REACH THE WIRE LASSO AND CUTS THROUGH. LUKE SHRUGS AWAY THE CABLE AND STANDS FREE.

ANOTHER BLAST FROM THE BARGE'S DECK GUN HITS NEAR BOBA AND HE IS KNOCKED UNCONSCIOUS TO THE DECK, NEXT TO WHERE LANDO IS HANGING.

LANDO

Han! Chewie?

HAN

Lando!

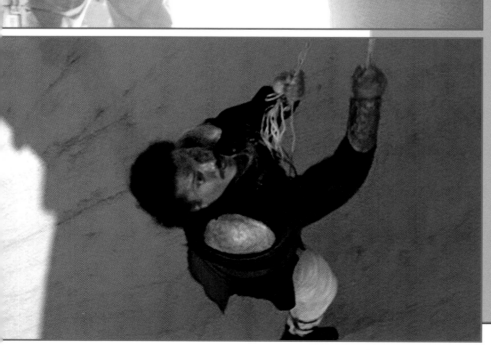

LUKE IS A LITTLE SHAKEN BUT
REMAINS STANDING AS A
FUSILLADE BRACKETS HIM. THE
SECOND SKIFF, LOADED WITH
GUARDS FIRING THEIR WEAPONS,
MOVES IN ON LUKE FAST. LUKE
LEAPS TOWARD THE INCOMING
SECOND SKIFF. THE YOUNG JEDI
LEAPS INTO THE MIDDLE OF THE
SECOND SKIFF AND BEGINS
DECIMATING THE GUARDS FROM
THEIR MIDST.

CHEWIE, WOUNDED, HAS BARKED
DIRECTIONS TO HAN, GUIDING HIM
TOWARD A SPEAR WHICH HAS
BEEN DROPPED BY ONE OF THE
GUARDS. FINALLY HAN GRABS
HOLD OF THE SPEAR.

BOBA FETT, BADLY SHAKEN, RISES
FROM THE DECK. HE LOOKS OVER
AT THE OTHER SKIFF, WHERE
LUKE IS WHIPPING A MASS OF
GUARDS. BOBA RAISES HIS ARM
AND AIMS HIS LETHAL
APPENDAGE.

CHEWIE BARKS DESPERATELY
AT HAN.

HAN

Boba Fett?! Where?

THE SPACE PIRATE TURNS
AROUND BLINDLY, AND THE
LONG SPEAR IN HIS HAND
WHACKS SQUARELY IN THE MIDDLE
OF BOBA'S ROCKET PACK.

THE IMPACT OF THE SWING CAUSES THE ROCKET PACK TO IGNITE. BOBA BLASTS OFF, FLYING OVER THE SECOND SKIFF LIKE A MISSILE, SMASHING AGAINST THE SIDE OF THE HUGE SAIL BARGE AND SLIDING AWAY INTO THE AIR. HE SCREAMS AS HIS ARMORED BODY MAKES ITS LAST FLIGHT PAST LANDO AND DIRECTLY INTO THE MUCOUS MOUTH OF THE SARLACC. THE SARLACC BURPS.

INTERIOR SAIL BARGE

LEIA WRECKS THE POWER SUPPLY, THROWING THE OBSERVATION DECK INTO DARKNESS, THEN LEAPS ON TO JABBA'S THRONE, AND THROWS THE CHAIN THAT ENSLAVES HER OVER HIS HEAD AROUND THE BULBOUS NECK. THEN SHE DIVES OFF THE OTHER SIDE OF THE THRONE, PULLING THE CHAIN VIOLENTLY IN HER GRASP. JABBA'S FLACCID NECK CONTRACTS BENEATH THE TIGHTENING CHAIN. HIS HUGE EYES BULGE FROM THEIR SOCKETS AND HIS SCUM-COATED TONGUE FLOPS OUT.

EXTERIOR SKIFF

LUKE CONTINUES TO DESTROY THE ALIENS ON THE GUARDS' SKIFF, AS HAN EXTENDS HIS SPEAR DOWNWARD TO LANDO, WHO IS STILL DANGLING PRECARIOUSLY FROM A ROPE ON THE PRISONERS' SKIFF.

HAN
___

Lando, grab it!

LANDO
___

Lower it!

HAN
___

I'm trying!

INTERIOR SAIL BARGE

THE EXALTED HUTT'S HUGE TAIL SPASMS THROUGH ITS DEATH THROES AND THEN SLAMS DOWN INTO FINAL STILLNESS.

EXTERIOR SKIFF

A MAJOR HIT FROM THE BARGE DECK GUN KNOCKS THE SKIFF ON ITS SIDE. HAN AND ALMOST EVERYTHING ELSE ON BOARD SLIDES OVERBOARD. THE ROPE BREAKS, AND LANDO FALLS TO THE SIDE OF THE SARLACC PIT. LUCKILY, HAN'S FOOT CATCHES ON THE SKIFF RAILING AND HE DANGLES ABOVE LANDO AND THE PIT. THE WOUNDED WOOKIEE HOLDS ONTO THE SKIFF FOR DEAR LIFE.

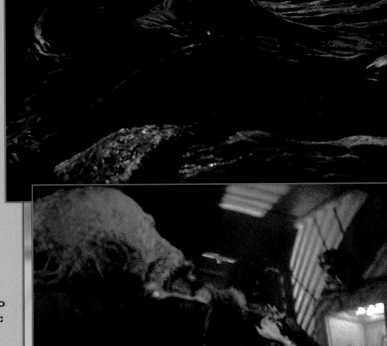

HAN
___

Whoa! Whoa! Whoa! Grab me, Chewie! I'm slipping.

CHEWIE GRABS HOLD OF HAN'S FEET, HOLDING HIM UPSIDE DOWN, AS HAN EXTENDS THE SPEAR TOWARD LANDO, WHO IS CLUTCHING TO THE SIDE OF THE PIT. LUKE HAS FINISHED OFF THE LAST GUARD ON THE SECOND SKIFF. HE SEES THE DECK GUN BLASTING AWAY AT HIS HELPLESS COMPANIONS.

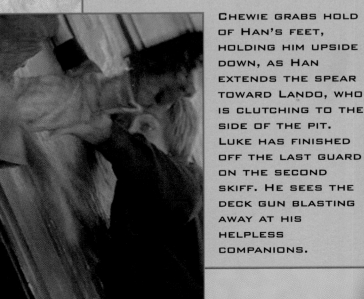

EXTERIOR UPPER DECK – SAIL BARGE

THE DECK GUNNER CONTINUES TO BLAST AWAY.

EXTERIOR SKIFF

LUKE LEAPS FROM THE SKIFF, ACROSS THE CHASM OF AIR, TO THE SHEER METALLIC SIDE OF THE SAIL BARGE. BARELY ABLE TO GET A FINGERHOLD, HE IS ABOUT TO BEGIN A PAINFUL CLIMB UP THE HULL, WHEN SUDDENLY AN ALIEN COMES THROUGH A HATCH INCHES FROM HIS HEAD. WITH JEDI AGILITY, LUKE GRASPS THE WRIST HOLDING THE GUN AND YANKS THE HELPLESS GUARD THROUGH THE HATCH AND INTO THE DEADLY PIT.

THE INJURED CHEWIE IS STILL REACHING OVER THE RAIL FOR THE DANGLING HAN, WHO IS, IN TURN, STILL BLINDLY REACHING DOWN TOWARD THE DESPERATE LANDO. THE BARON HAS STOPPED HIS SLIPPAGE DOWN THE SANDY SLOPE OF THE SARLACC PIT BY LYING VERY STILL.

HAN

Grab it! Almost…You almost got it!

EXTERIOR UPPER DECK – SAIL BARGE

THE DECK GUNNER FIRES AGAIN.

EXTERIOR SKIFF

THE BLAST HITS THE FRONT OF THE TILTED SKIFF, CAUSING LANDO TO LET GO OF THE SPEAR.

LANDO

Hold it! Whoa!

EXTERIOR UPPER DECK

THE DECK GUNNERS HAVE CHEWIE AND THE DESPERATE DANGLING HUMAN CHAIN IN THE GUN SIGHTS WHEN SOMETHING UP ON DECK COMMANDS THEIR ATTENTION. LUKE, STANDING BEFORE THEM LIKE A PIRATE KING, IGNITES HIS LIGHTSABER. THE DECK GUNNERS HAVE BARELY REACHED FOR THEIR PISTOLS BEFORE THE YOUNG JEDI HAS DEMOLISHED THEM.

EXTERIOR SKIFF

AGAIN HAN EXTENDS THE SPEAR TOWARD LANDO.

HAN

Gently now. All…all right. Easy. Hold me, Chewie.

LANDO SCREAMS. ONE OF THE SARLACC'S TENTACLES HAS WRAPPED TIGHTLY AROUND HIS ANKLE, DRAGGING HIM DOWN THE SIDE OF THE PIT.

HAN

Chewie!

EXTERIOR UPPER DECK – SAIL BARGE

LUKE CONTINUES TO HOLD THE UPPER DECK AGAINST ALL COMERS.

EXTERIOR SKIFF

HAN

Chewie, give me the gun. Don't move, Lando.

LANDO

No, wait! I thought you were blind!

HAN

It's all right. Trust me. Don't move.

LANDO

A little higher! Just a little higher!

HAN ADJUSTS HIS AIM AS LANDO LOWERS HIS HEAD, AND THE FUZZY-EYED PIRATE FIRES AT THE TENTACLE. DIRECT HIT. THE TENTACLE RELEASES LANDO.

HAN

Chewie, pull us up! All right...up, Chewie, up!

CHEWIE STARTS TO PULL THEM ON BOARD THE SKIFF.

INTERIOR SAIL BARGE – OBSERVATION DECK

ARTOO EXTENDS A SMALL LASER GUN AND BLASTS LEIA'S CHAIN APART.

LEIA

Come on. We gotta get out of here.

ARTOO AND LEIA RACE FOR THE EXIT, PASSING THREEPIO, WHO IS KICKING AND SCREAMING AS SALACIOUS CRUMB, THE REPTILIAN MONKEY-MONSTER, PICKS OUT ONE OF THE GOLDEN DROID'S EYES.

THREEPIO

Not my eye! Artoo, help! Quickly, Artoo. Oh! Ohhh!

ARTOO ZIPS OVER AND ZAPS SALACIOUS, SENDING HIM SKYWARD WITH A SCREAM, INTO THE RAFTERS.

THREEPIO

Beast!

EXTERIOR SKIFF

ON BOARD THE SKIFF, CHEWIE AND LANDO ARE HELPING HAN UP.

EXTERIOR UPPER DECK – SAIL BARGE

LUKE IS WARDING OFF LASER BLASTS WITH HIS LIGHTSABER, SURROUNDED BY GUARDS AND FIGHTING LIKE A DEMON. LEIA EMERGES ON TO THE DECK AS LUKE TURNS TO FACE ANOTHER GUARD.

LUKE (TO LEIA)

Get the gun! Point it at the deck!

LEIA TURNS TOWARDS THE BARGE CANNON, CLIMBS ON THE PLATFORM, AND SWIVELS THE GUN AROUND.

LUKE

Point it at the deck!

A LASER BLAST HITS LUKE'S MECHANICAL HAND AND HE BENDS OVER IN PAIN, BUT HE MANAGES TO SWING HIS LIGHTSABER UPWARD AND TAKE OUT THE LAST OF THE GUARDS.

Near the rail of the upper deck, Artoo and Threepio steady themselves as Threepio gets ready to jump. Artoo beeps wildly.

THREEPIO

Artoo, where are we going? I couldn't possibly jump...

Artoo butts the golden droid over the edge and steps off himself, tumbling toward the sand.

Luke runs along the empty deck toward Leia and the barge gun, which she has brought around to point down at the deck.

LUKE

Come on!

Luke has hold of one of the rigging ropes from the mast. He gathers Leia in his other arm and kicks the trigger of the deck gun.

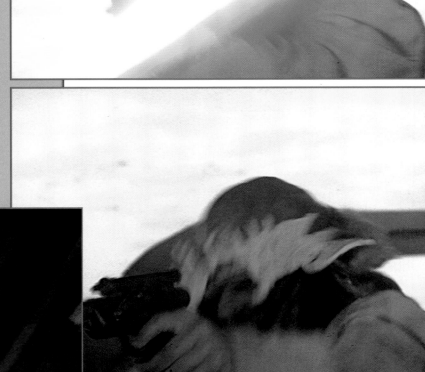

THE GUN EXPLODES INTO THE DECK AS
LUKE AND LEIA SWING OUT TOWARD
THE SKIFF.

EXTERIOR SKIFF

HAN IS TENDING TO THE WOUNDED
CHEWIE AS LUKE AND LEIA LAND ON
THE SKIFF WITH FLAIR.

LUKE

Let's go! And don't forget the droids.

LANDO

We're on our way.

THE SAIL BARGE IS EXPLODING IN
STAGES IN THE DISTANCE. HALF OF
THE HUGE CRAFT IS ON FIRE.

EXTERIOR SAND DUNE

ARTOO'S PERISCOPE STICKS UP FROM
THE DUNE WHERE HE LANDED. NEXT
TO IT, THREEPIO'S LEGS ARE THE ONLY
THINGS ABOVE SAND. AS THE SKIFF
FLOATS ABOVE THEM, TWO LARGE
ELECTROMAGNETS DANGLE DOWN ON A
WIRE. BOTH DROIDS ARE PULLED FROM
THE SAND.

EXTERIOR DUNE SEA.

The burning sail barge continues its chain of explosions. As the skiff sails off across the desert, the barge settles to the sand and disappears in one final conflagration.

EXTERIOR SPACE ABOVE TATOOINE

The desolate yellow planet fills the screen. The Falcon appears and grows huge, to roar directly over camera, followed by Luke's X-wing, which peels off to the left.

INTERIOR X-WING — COCKPIT

Luke is at the controls. He speaks into his comlink to the others, in the Millennium Falcon.

LUKE

Meet you back at the fleet.

LEIA (OVER COMLINK)

Hurry. The Alliance should be assembled by now.

LUKE

I will.

HAN (OVER COMLINK)

Hey, Luke, thanks. Thanks for comin' after me. Now I owe you one.

EXTERIOR X-WING

Artoo, who is attached to Luke's X-wing outside the canopy, beeps a message.

INTERIOR X-WING — COCKPIT

The message from Artoo appears on the small monitor screen in front of Luke. He smiles at the monitor and speaks to Artoo, as he pulls a black glove on to cover his wounded mechanical hand.

LUKE

That's right, Artoo. We're going to the Dagobah system. I have a promise to keep...to an old friend.

EXTERIOR SPACE

LUKE'S X-WING SOARS OFF.

EXTERIOR DEATH STAR

SQUADS OF TIE FIGHTERS ESCORT AN
IMPERIAL SHUTTLE TOWARD THE
HALF-COMPLETED DEATH STAR.

INTERIOR DEATH STAR – DOCKING BAY

THOUSANDS OF IMPERIAL TROOPS IN TIGHT
FORMATION FILL THE MAMMOTH DOCKING
BAY. VADER AND THE DEATH STAR
COMMANDER WAIT AT THE LANDING
PLATFORM, WHERE THE SHUTTLE HAS COME
TO REST.

THE EMPEROR'S ROYAL
GUARDS COME DOWN THE
SHUTTLE'S RAMP AND CREATE
A LETHAL PERIMETER. THEN,
IN THE HUGE SILENCE WHICH
FOLLOWS, THE EMPEROR
APPEARS. HE IS A RATHER
SMALL, SHRIVELED OLD MAN.
HIS BENT FRAME SLOWLY
MAKES ITS WAY DOWN THE
RAMP WITH THE AID OF A
GNARLED CANE. HE WEARS A
HOODED CLOAK SIMILAR TO
THE ONE BEN WEARS, EXCEPT
THAT IT IS BLACK. THE
EMPEROR'S FACE IS
SHROUDED AND DIFFICULT TO
SEE. COMMANDER JERJERROD
AND DARTH VADER ARE
KNEELING TO HIM.

EMPEROR (TO VADER)

Rise, my friend.

THE SUPREME RULER OF THE
GALAXY BECKONS TO THE
DARK LORD.

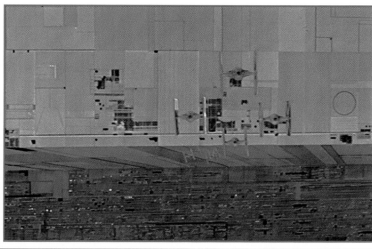

047

VADER RISES, AND FALLS IN NEXT TO THE
EMPEROR AS HE SLOWLY MAKES HIS WAY
ALONG THE ROWS OF TROOPS. JERJERROD
AND THE OTHER COMMANDERS WILL STAY
KNEELING UNTIL THE SUPREME RULER AND
VADER, FOLLOWED BY SEVERAL IMPERIAL
DIGNITARIES, PASS BY; ONLY THEN DO THEY
JOIN IN THE PROCESSION.

VADER

The Death Star will be completed on schedule.

EMPEROR

You have done well, Lord Vader. And now I sense you
wish to continue your search for young Skywalker.

VADER

Yes, my Master.

EMPEROR

Patience, my friend. In time he will seek you out. And
when he does, you must bring him before me. He has
grown strong. Only together can we turn him to the
dark side of the Force.

VADER

As you wish.

EMPEROR

Everything is proceeding as I have foreseen.

HE LAUGHS TO HIMSELF AS THEY PASS
ALONG THE VAST LINE OF IMPERIAL
TROOPS.

EXTERIOR YODA'S HOUSE – DAGOBAH

ONCE AGAIN, ARTOO FINDS HIMSELF
WAITING AROUND IN THE DAMP ENVIRONS OF
THE SWAMP PLANET, AND HE'S NONE TOO
HAPPY ABOUT IT. HE BEEPS
DISCONSOLATELY TO HIMSELF AND TURNS
TO LOOK AT YODA'S COTTAGE. WARM
YELLOW LIGHT ESCAPES THE ODDLY SHAPED
WINDOWS TO FIGHT THE GLOOM.

INTERIOR YODA'S HOUSE

A WALKING STICK TAPS HESITANTLY ACROSS
THE EARTHEN FLOOR OF THE COTTAGE. THE
SMALL GREEN HAND THAT CLUTCHES IT IS
FOLLOWED BY THE FAMILIAR FACE OF YODA,
THE JEDI MASTER. HIS MANNER IS FRAIL,
AND HIS VOICE, THOUGH CHEERFUL, SEEMS
WEAKER.

YODA

Hmm. That face you make? Look I so old to young
eyes?

LUKE IS SITTING IN A CORNER OF THE CRAMPED SPACE AND, INDEED, HIS LOOK HAS BEEN WOEFUL. CAUGHT, HE TRIES TO HIDE IT.

LUKE

No...of course not.

YODA (TICKLED, CHUCKLES)

I do, yes, I do! Sick have I become. Old and weak.

(POINTS A CROOKED FINGER)

When nine hundred years old you reach, look as good you will not. Hmm?

YODA CHUCKLES AT THIS, COUGHS, AND HOBBLES OVER TOWARD HIS BED.

YODA

Soon will I rest. Yes, for ever sleep. Earned it, I have.

YODA SITS HIMSELF ON HIS BED, WITH GREAT EFFORT.

LUKE

Master Yoda, you can't die.

YODA

Strong I am with the Force...but not that strong! Twilight is upon me and soon night must fall. That is the way of things...the way of the Force.

LUKE

But I need your help. I've come back to complete the training.

YODA

No more training do you require. Already know you that which you need.

YODA SIGHS, LYING BACK ON HIS BED.

LUKE

Then I am a Jedi.

YODA (SHAKES HIS HEAD)

Ohhh. Not yet. One thing remains: Vader. You must confront Vader. Then, only then, a Jedi will you be. And confront him you will.

LUKE IS IN AGONY. HE IS SILENT FOR A MOMENT, SCREWING UP HIS COURAGE. FINALLY HE IS ABLE TO ASK.

LUKE

Master Yoda...is Darth Vader my father?

YODA'S EYES ARE FULL OF WEARINESS AND COMPASSION. AN ODD, SAD SMILE CREASES HIS FACE. HE TURNS PAINFULLY ON HIS SIDE, AWAY FROM LUKE.

YODA

Mmm...rest I need. Yes...rest.

LUKE WATCHES HIM, EACH MOMENT AN ETERNITY.

LUKE

Yoda, I must know.

YODA

Your father he is. Told you, did he?

LUKE

Yes.

A NEW LOOK OF CONCERN CROSSES YODA'S FACE. HE CLOSES HIS EYES.

YODA

Unexpected this is, and unfortunate...

LUKE

Unfortunate that I know the truth?

YODA OPENS HIS EYES AGAIN AND STUDIES THE YOUTH.

YODA
(GATHERING ALL HIS STRENGTH)

Unfortunate that you rushed to face him...that incomplete was your training. That not ready for the burden were you.

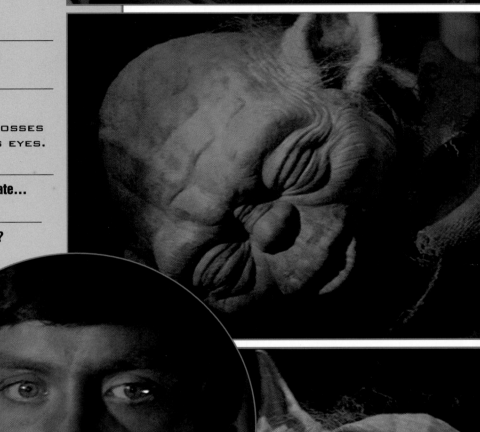

LUKE

I'm sorry.

YODA

Remember, a Jedi's strength flows from the Force. But beware. Anger, fear, aggression. The dark side are they. Once you start down the dark path, forever will it dominate your destiny.

(FAINTLY)

Luke...Luke...

THE YOUNG JEDI MOVES CLOSER TO HIM.

YODA

Do not...Do not underestimate the powers of the Emperor, or suffer your father's fate, you will. Luke, when gone am I...the last of the Jedi will you be. Luke, the Force runs strong in your family. Pass on what you have learned, Luke...

(WITH GREAT EFFORT)

There is...another...Sky...walker.

THE ANCIENT GREEN CREATURE CATCHES HIS BREATH AND DIES. LUKE STARES AT HIS DEAD MASTER AS HE DISAPPEARS IN FRONT OF HIS EYES.

EXTERIOR DAGOBAH SWAMP – X-WING

LUKE WANDERS BACK TO WHERE HIS SHIP IS SITTING. ARTOO BEEPS A GREETING, BUT IS IGNORED BY HIS DEPRESSED MASTER. LUKE KNEELS DOWN, BEGINS TO HELP ARTOO WITH THE SHIP, THEN STOPS AND SHAKES HIS HEAD DEJECTEDLY.

LUKE

I can't do it, Artoo. I can't go on alone.

BEN (OFFSCREEN)

Yoda will always be with you.

051

LUKE LOOKS UP TO SEE THE
SHIMMERING IMAGE OF BEN
KENOBI.

LUKE

Obi-Wan!

THE GHOST OF BEN KENOBI
APPROACHES HIM THROUGH THE
SWAMP.

LUKE

Why didn't you tell me? You told me
Vader betrayed and murdered my father.

BEN

Your father was seduced by the dark side
of the Force. He ceased to be Anakin
Skywalker and became Darth Vader.
When that happened, the good man who
was your father was destroyed. So what I
told you was true...from a certain point of
view.

LUKE (DERISIVE)

A certain point of view!

BEN

Luke, you're going to find that many of
the truths we cling to depend greatly
on our own point of view.

LUKE IS UNRESPONSIVE. BEN
STUDIES HIM IN SILENCE FOR A
MOMENT.

BEN

Anakin was a good friend.

AS BEN SPEAKS, LUKE SETTLES
ON A STUMP, MESMERIZED.

BEN

When I first knew him, your father was
already a great pilot. But I was amazed
how strongly the Force was with him. I
took it upon myself to train him as a Jedi.
I thought that I could instruct him just as
well as Yoda. I was wrong.

LUKE IS ENTRANCED.

LUKE

There is still good in him.

BEN

He's more machine now than man. Twisted and evil.

LUKE

I can't do it, Ben.

BEN

You cannot escape your destiny. You must face Darth Vader again.

LUKE

I can't kill my own father.

BEN

Then the Emperor has already won. You were our only hope.

LUKE

Yoda spoke of another.

BEN

The other he spoke of is your twin sister.

LUKE

But I have no sister.

BEN

Hmm. To protect you both from the Emperor, you were hidden from your father when you were born. The Emperor knew, as I did, if Anakin were to have any offspring, they would be a threat to him. That is the reason why your sister remains safely anonymous.

LUKE

Leia! Leia's my sister.

BEN

Your insight serves you well. Bury your feelings deep down, Luke. They do you credit. But they could be made to serve the Emperor.

LUKE LOOKS INTO THE DISTANCE, TRYING TO COMPREHEND ALL THIS.

053

EXTERIOR SPACE – REBEL FLEET

THE VAST REBEL FLEET STRETCHES AS FAR AS THE EYE CAN SEE. OVERHEAD A DOZEN SMALL CORELLIAN BATTLESHIPS FLY IN FORMATION. FIGHTERS AND BATTLECRUISERS SURROUND THE LARGEST OF THE REBEL STAR CRUISERS, THE HEADQUARTERS FRIGATE.

INTERIOR HEADQUARTERS FRIGATE – MAIN BRIEFING ROOM

HUNDREDS OF REBEL COMMANDERS OF ALL RACES AND FORMS ARE ASSEMBLING IN THE WAR ROOM. WEDGE IS AMONG THEM. IN THE CENTER OF THE ROOM IS A HOLOGRAPHIC MODEL DEPICTING THE HALF-COMPLETED IMPERIAL DEATH STAR, THE NEARBY MOON OF ENDOR, AND THE PROTECTING DEFLECTOR SHIELD.

Moving through the crowd, Han finds Lando. He peers at Lando's new insignia on his chest, and is amused.

HAN

Well, look at you, a general, huh?

LANDO

Someone must have told them about my little maneuver at the battle of Taanab.

HAN (SARCASTIC)

Well, don't look at me, pal. I just said you were a fair pilot. I didn't know they were lookin' for somebody to lead this crazy attack.

LANDO (SMILING)

I'm surprised they didn't ask you to do it.

HAN

Well, who says they didn't? But I ain't crazy. You're the respectable one, remember?

Mon Mothma, the leader of the Alliance, has entered the room. She is a stern but beautiful woman in her fifties. Mon Mothma signals for attention, and the room falls silent.

MON MOTHMA

The Emperor has made a critical error and the time for our attack has come.

THIS CAUSES A STIR. MON MOTHMA TURNS TO A HOLOGRAPHIC MODEL OF THE DEATH STAR, THE NEARBY ENDOR MOON AND THE PROTECTING DEFLECTOR SHIELD IN THE CENTER OF THE ROOM.

MON MOTHMA

The data brought to us by the Bothan spies pinpoints the exact location of the Emperor's new battle station. We also know that the weapon systems of this Death Star are not yet operational. With the Imperial fleet spread throughout the galaxy in a vain effort to engage us, it is relatively unprotected. But most important of all, we've learned that the Emperor himself is personally overseeing the final stages of the construction of this Death Star. Many Bothans died to bring us this information. Admiral Ackbar, please.

ADMIRAL ACKBAR (A SALMON-COLORED MON CALAMARI) STEPS FORWARD, INDICATING THE DEATH STAR'S FORCE FIELD AND THE MOON OF ENDOR.

ACKBAR

You can see here the Death Star orbiting the forest Moon of Endor. Although the weapon systems on this Death Star are not yet operational, the Death Star does have a strong defense mechanism. It is protected by an energy shield, which is generated from the nearby forest Moon of Endor. The shield must be deactivated if any attack is to be attempted. Once the shield is down, our cruisers will create a perimeter, while the fighters fly into the superstructure and attempt to knock out the main reactor. General Calrissian has volunteered to lead the fighter attack.

HAN TURNS TO LANDO WITH A LOOK OF RESPECT.

HAN

Good luck.

LANDO RETURNS HIS LOOK.

HAN

You're gonna need it.

ACKBAR

General Madine.

MADINE MOVES CENTER STAGE.

GENERAL MADINE

We have stolen a small Imperial shuttle. Disguised as a cargo ship, and using a secret Imperial code, a strike team will land on the moon and deactivate the shield generator.

THE ASSEMBLY BEGINS TO MUMBLE AMONG THEMSELVES.

THREEPIO

Sounds dangerous.

LEIA (TO HAN)

I wonder who they found to pull that off.

GENERAL MADINE

General Solo, is your strike team assembled?

LEIA, STARTLED, LOOKS UP AT HAN, SURPRISE CHANGING TO ADMIRATION.

HAN

Uh, my team's ready. I don't have a command crew for the shuttle.

CHEWBACCA RAISES HIS HAIRY PAW AND VOLUNTEERS. HAN LOOKS UP AT HIM.

HAN

Well, it's gonna be rough, pal. I didn't want to speak for you.

CHEWIE WAVES THAT OFF WITH A HUGE GROWL.

HAN (SMILES)

That's one.

LEIA

Uh, General...count me in.

VOICE (OFFSCREEN)

I'm with you, too!

THEY TURN IN THAT DIRECTION
AND PEER INTO THE CROWD,
WHICH PARTS TO ADMIT LUKE.
HAN AND LEIA ARE SURPRISED
AND DELIGHTED.

LEIA MOVES TO LUKE AND
EMBRACES HIM WARMLY. SHE
SENSES A CHANGE IN HIM AND
LOOKS INTO HIS EYES
QUESTIONINGLY.

LEIA

What is it?

LUKE (HESITANT)

Ask me again sometime.

HAN, CHEWIE AND LANDO CROWD
AROUND LUKE AS THE ASSEMBLY
BREAKS UP.

HAN

Luke.

LUKE

Hi, Han…Chewie.

ARTOO BEEPS A SINGSONG
OBSERVATION TO A WORRIED
THREEPIO.

THREEPIO

'Exciting' is hardly the word I would choose.

INTERIOR HEADQUARTERS
FRIGATE – MAIN DOCKING BAY

THE MILLENNIUM FALCON
RESTS BEYOND THE STOLEN
IMPERIAL SHUTTLE, WHICH
LOOKS ANOMALOUS AMONG ALL
THE REBEL SHIPS IN THE VAST
DOCKING BAY CROWDED NOW
WITH THE REBEL STRIKE TEAM
LOADING WEAPONS AND
SUPPLIES. LANDO TURNS TO
FACE HAN.

HAN

Look: I want you to take her. I mean it.
Take her. You need all the help you
can get. She's the fastest ship in the fleet.

LANDO

All right, old buddy. You know, I know what
she means to you. I'll take good care of her.
She – she won't get a scratch. All right?

HAN

Right. I got your promise. Not a scratch.

LANDO

Look, would you get going, you pirate.

HAN AND LANDO PAUSE, THEN EXCHANGE
SALUTES.

LANDO

Good luck.

HAN

You too.

HAN GOES UP THE RAMP. LANDO WATCHES
HIM GO AND THEN SLOWLY TURNS AWAY.

INTERIOR IMPERIAL SHUTTLE – COCKPIT

LUKE IS WORKING ON A BACK CONTROL
PANEL AS HAN COMES IN AND TAKES THE
PILOT'S SEAT. CHEWIE, IN THE SEAT NEXT
TO HIM, IS TRYING TO FIGURE OUT ALL THE
IMPERIAL CONTROLS.

HAN

You got her warmed?

LUKE

Yeah, she's comin' up.

CHEWIE GROWLS A COMPLAINT.

HAN

I don't think the Empire had Wookiees in mind when
they designed her, Chewie.

INTERIOR HEADQUARTERS
FRIGATE – MAIN DOCKING BAY

THE SHUTTLE WARMS UP.

INTERIOR IMPERIAL SHUTTLE – COCKPIT

LEIA COMES IN FROM THE HOLD
AND PUTS A HAND ON HAN'S
SHOULDER.

HAN'S GLANCE HAS STUCK ON
SOMETHING OUT THE WINDOW: THE
MILLENNIUM FALCON. LEIA NUDGES
HIM GENTLY.

LEIA

Hey, are you awake?

HAN

Yeah. I just got a funny feeling. Like I'm not
gonna see her again.

CHEWIE, ON HEARING THIS, STOPS HIS
ACTIVITY AND LOOKS LONGINGLY OUT
AT THE FALCON, TOO.

LEIA (SOFTLY)

Come on, General, let's move.

HAN SNAPS BACK TO LIFE.

HAN

Right. Chewie, let's see what this piece of junk
can do. Ready, everybody?

LUKE

All set.

THREEPIO

Here we go again.

EXTERIOR SPACE – THE REBEL FLEET

THE STOLEN IMPERIAL SHUTTLE LEAVES
THE MAIN DOCKING BAY OF THE
HEADQUARTERS FRIGATE, AND
LOWERS ITS WINGS INTO FLIGHT
POSITION.

INTERIOR IMPERIAL SHUTTLE – COCKPIT

HAN

All right, hang on.

EXTERIOR SPACE – THE REBEL FLEET

THE IMPERIAL SHUTTLE ZOOMS OFF
INTO SPACE.

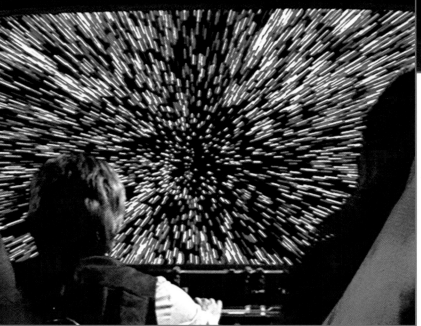

EXTERIOR SPACE – DEATH STAR

TIE FIGHTERS PATROL THE SURFACE OF THE
DEATH STAR.

INTERIOR EMPEROR'S THRONE ROOM

THE CONVERTED CONTROL ROOM IS DIMLY
LIT. THE EMPEROR STANDS BEFORE A LARGE
WINDOW WHICH LOOKS OUT ACROSS THE
HALF-COMPLETED DEATH STAR TO THE
GIANT GREEN MOON OF ENDOR.

DARTH VADER STANDS WITH OTHER
MEMBERS OF THE IMPERIAL COUNCIL. THE
RULER'S BACK IS TO VADER.

VADER

What is thy bidding, my Master?

EMPEROR (TURNING)

Send the fleet to the far side of Endor. There it will
stay until called for.

VADER

What of the reports of the Rebel fleet massing near
Sullust?

EMPEROR

It is of no concern. Soon the Rebellion will be crushed
and young Skywalker will be one of us! Your work
  here is finished, my friend. Go out to the command
  ship and await my orders.

VADER

Yes, my Master.

VADER BOWS, THEN TURNS AND EXITS THE
THRONE ROOM AS THE EMPEROR WALKS
TOWARD THE WAITING COUNCIL MEMBERS.

EXTERIOR SPACE – DEATH STAR – MOON

THE IMPERIAL SHUTTLE APPROACHES THE DEATH STAR.

INTERIOR STOLEN IMPERIAL SHUTTLE – COCKPIT

THERE IS A GREAT DEAL OF IMPERIAL TRAFFIC IN THE AREA AS CONSTRUCTION PROCEEDS ON THE DEATH STAR. TIE FIGHTERS AND A FEW STAR DESTROYERS MOVE ABOUT.

AS CHEWIE FLIPS SWITCHES, THROUGH THE VIEWSCREEN, THE DEATH STAR AND THE HUGE SUPER STAR DESTROYER CAN BE SEEN.

HAN
<hr/>
If they don't go for this, we're gonna have to get outta here pretty quick, Chewie.

CHEWIE GROWLS HIS AGREEMENT.

CONTROLLER (OVER RADIO)
<hr/>
We have you on our screen now. Please identify.

HAN
<hr/>
Shuttle Tydirium requesting deactivation of the deflector shield.

EXTERIOR SPACE – DEATH STAR – MOON

THE SHUTTLE APPROACHES THE SUPER STAR DESTROYER.

INTERIOR SUPER STAR DESTROYER – BRIDGE

CONTROLLER (INTO RADIO)
<hr/>
Shuttle Tydirium, transmit the clearance code for shield passage.

INTERIOR STOLEN IMPERIAL SHUTTLE – COCKPIT

HAN
<hr/>
Transmission commencing.

LEIA
<hr/>
Now we find out if that code is worth the price we paid.

HAN
<hr/>
It'll work. It'll work.

CHEWIE WHINES NERVOUSLY. THEY LISTEN TENSELY AS THE SOUND OF A HIGH SPEED TRANSMISSION BEGINS. LUKE STARES AT THE HUGE SUPER STAR DESTROYER THAT LOOMS EVER LARGER BEFORE THEM.

LUKE

Vader's on that ship.

HAN

Now don't get jittery, Luke. There are a lot of command ships. Keep your distance though, Chewie, but don't look like you're trying to keep your distance.

CHEWIE BARKS A QUESTION.

HAN

I don't know. Fly casual.

CHEWIE BARKS HIS WORRIES AS THE SUPER STAR DESTROYER GROWS LARGER OUT THE WINDOW.

INTERIOR VADER'S STAR DESTROYER – BRIDGE

LORD VADER WALKS DOWN THE ROW OF CONTROLLERS TO WHERE ADMIRAL PIETT IS LOOKING OVER THE TRACKING SCREEN OF THE CONTROLLER WE'VE SEEN EARLIER. PIETT LOOKS AROUND AT VADER'S APPROACH.

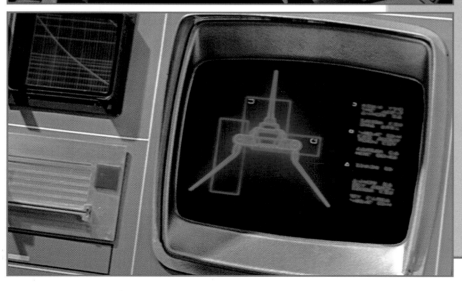

VADER

Where is that shuttle going?

PIETT (INTO COMLINK)

Shuttle Tydirium, what is your cargo and destination?

PILOT VOICE (HAN) (FILTERED)

Parts and technical crew for the forest moon.

THE BRIDGE COMMANDER LOOKS TO VADER FOR A REACTION.

VADER

Do they have code clearance?

PIETT

It's an older code, sir, but it checks out. I was about to clear them.

VADER LOOKS UPWARD, AS HE SENSES LUKE'S PRESENCE.

INTERIOR STOLEN IMPERIAL
SHUTTLE – COCKPIT

LUKE

I'm endangering the mission. I shouldn't have
come.

HAN

It's your imagination, kid. Come on. Let's keep
a little optimism here.

EXTERIOR SPACE – STOLEN
IMPERIAL SHUTTLE – DEATH STAR

THE SHUTTLE CONTINUES ON ITS WAY.

INTERIOR VADER'S STAR DESTROYER – BRIDGE

PIETT

Shall I hold them?

VADER

No. Leave them to me. I will deal with them myself.

PIETT (SURPRISED)

As you wish, My Lord.

(TO CONTROLLER)

Carry on.

INTERIOR STOLEN IMPERIAL
SHUTTLE – COCKPIT

THE GROUP WAITS TENSELY.

HAN

They're not goin' for it, Chewie.

CONTROLLER (FILTERED)

Shuttle Tydirium, deactivation of
the shield will commence
immediately. Follow your present
course.

EVERYONE BREATHES A SIGH
OF RELIEF. EVERYONE BUT
LUKE, WHO LOOKS WORRIED.

HAN

Okay! I told you it was gonna work.
No problem.

EXTERIOR SPACE – STOLEN
IMPERIAL SHUTTLE – ENDOR

THE STOLEN IMPERIAL
SHUTTLE MOVES OFF
TOWARD THE GREEN
SANCTUARY MOON.

INTERIOR VADER'S STAR
DESTROYER – BRIDGE

VADER WATCHES FROM
THE BRIDGE.

EXTERIOR ENDOR – FOREST
CANOPY

THE SHUTTLE COMES IN
TO LAND.

EXTERIOR FOREST
LANDING SITE – ENDOR

IN THE MOON'S DARK PRIMEVAL
FOREST, DWARFED BY THE
ANCIENT, TOWERING TREES, THE
HELMETED REBEL CONTINGENT
MAKES ITS WAY UP THE STEEP
TRAIL. LEIA AND HAN ARE
SLIGHTLY AHEAD OF LUKE AND
CHEWIE. THE TROOPS OF THE
STRIKE-TEAM SQUAD FOLLOW, WITH
ARTOO AND THREEPIO BRINGING
UP THE REAR.

UP AHEAD, HAN AND LEIA REACH
A CREST IN THE HILL AND DROP
SUDDENLY TO THE GROUND,
SIGNALING THE REST OF THE
GROUP TO STOP.

THREEPIO

Oh, I told you it was dangerous here.

THEIR P.O.V: NOT FAR BELOW
THEM, TWO IMPERIAL SCOUTS ARE
WANDERING THROUGH BUSHES IN
THE VALLEY BELOW. THEIR TWO
ROCKET BIKES ARE PARKED
NEARBY.

LEIA

Should we try and go around?

HAN

It'll take time. This whole party'll be for nothing if they see us. Chewie and I will take care of this. You stay here.

LUKE

Quietly, there might be more of them out there.

HAN (GRINS)

Hey…it's me.

HAN AND CHEWIE TURN AND START THROUGH THE BUSHES TOWARD THE SCOUTS. LUKE AND LEIA EXCHANGE SMILES.

066

HAN SNEAKS UP BEHIND ONE OF THE
SCOUTS, STEPS ON A TWIG AND THE SCOUT
WHIRLS, KNOCKING HAN INTO A TREE. THE
SCOUT SHOUTS FOR HIS COMPANION.

SCOUT #1

Go for help! Go!

LUKE (SARCASTIC)

Great. Come on.

THE SECOND SCOUT JUMPS ON HIS
SPEEDER BIKE AND TAKES OFF, BUT CHEWIE
GETS OFF A SHOT ON HIS CROSSBOW LASER
WEAPON, CAUSING THE SCOUT TO CRASH
INTO A TREE. HAN AND SCOUT #1 ARE IN A
ROUSING FISTFIGHT.

Luke starts for the scuffle, followed by Leia. As they run through the bushes, Leia stops and points to where two more scouts are sitting on their speeder bikes, with an unoccupied bike parked nearby.

LEIA

Over there! Two more of them!

LUKE

I see them. Wait, Leia!

But Leia doesn't hear him and races for the remaining speeder bike. She starts it up and takes off as Luke jumps on the bike behind her.

Luke and Leia speed into the dense foliage in hot pursuit, barely avoiding two huge trees.

HAN
─────────────────────────

Hey, wait! Ahhh!

He flips the remaining scout to the ground.

LUKE (POINTING
TO THE CONTROLS)
─────────────────────────

Quick! Jam their comlink. Center switch!

EXTERIOR FOREST – THE BIKE CHASE

The two fleeing Imperial scouts have a good lead as Luke and Leia pursue through the giant trees at 200 miles an hour.

LUKE

Move closer!

LEIA GUNS IT, CLOSING THE GAP, AS THE TWO SCOUTS RECKLESSLY VEER THROUGH A NARROW GAP IN THE TREES.

LUKE

Get alongside that one!

LEIA PULLS HER SPEEDER BIKE UP SO CLOSE TO THE SCOUT'S BIKE THAT THEY SCRAPE NOISILY. LUKE LEAPS FROM HIS BIKE TO THE BACK OF THE SCOUT'S, GRABS THE IMPERIAL WARRIOR AROUND THE NECK, AND FLIPS HIM OFF. THE BIKE, INTO A THICK TREE TRUNK. LUKE GAINS CONTROL OF THE BIKE AND FOLLOWS LEIA, WHO HAS PULLED AHEAD. THEY TEAR OFF AFTER THE REMAINING SCOUT.

THE SPEEDING CHASE PASSES TWO MORE
IMPERIAL SCOUTS. THESE TWO
SWING INTO PURSUIT, CHASING
LUKE AND LEIA, FIRING AWAY
WITH THEIR LASER CANNON. THE
TWO REBELS LOOK BEHIND THEM
JUST AS LUKE'S BIKE TAKES A
GLANCING HIT.

LUKE (INDICATING
THE ONE AHEAD)

Keep on that one! I'll take these two!

WITH LEIA SHOOTING AHEAD,
LUKE SUDDENLY SLAMS INTO
BRAKING MODE. LUKE'S BIKE IS A
BLUR TO THE TWO PURSUING
SCOUTS AS THEY ZIP BY HIM ON
EITHER SIDE. LUKE SLAMS HIS
BIKE INTO FORWARD AND STARTS
FIRING AWAY, HAVING SWITCHED
PLACES WITH HIS PURSUERS IN A
MATTER OF SECONDS.

Luke's aim is good and one scout's bike is blasted out of control. It explodes against a tree trunk.

The scout's cohort takes one glance back at the flash and shifts into turbo drive, going even faster. Luke keeps on his tail.

Far ahead, Leia and the first scout are doing a high-speed slalom through the death-dealing trunks. Now Leia aims her bike skyward and rises out of sight.

The scout turns in confusion, unable to see his pursuer. Suddenly, Leia dives down upon him from above, cannon blasting.

Leia moves in alongside him. The scout eyes her beside him, reaches down, and pulls out a handgun. Before Leia can react, the scout has blasted her bike, sending it out of control.

073

THE HAPPY SCOUT
LOOKS BACK AT THE
EXPLOSION. BUT
WHEN HE TURNS
FORWARD AGAIN, HE
IS ON A COLLISION
COURSE WITH A
GIANT FALLEN TREE.
HE HITS HIS BRAKES
TO NO AVAIL AND
DISAPPEARS IN A
CONFLAGRATION.

ANOTHER PART
OF THE FOREST:
LUKE AND THE LAST
REMAINING SCOUT
CONTINUE THEIR
WEAVING CHASE
THROUGH THE
TREES.

NOW LUKE MOVES UP CLOSE. THE SCOUT
RESPONDS BY SLAMMING HIS BIKE INTO
LUKE'S.

BOTH RIDERS LOOK AHEAD — A WIDE TRUNK
LOOMS DIRECTLY IN LUKE'S PATH, BUT THE
SCOUT'S BIKE BESIDE HIM MAKES IT ALMOST
IMPOSSIBLE FOR HIM TO
AVOID IT. LUKE REACTS
INSTINCTIVELY AND DIVES
OFF THE BIKE. IT EXPLODES
AGAINST THE TREE. THE
SCOUT SWEEPS OUT AND
CIRCLES BACK TO FIND
LUKE.

LUKE RISES FROM THE UNDERGROWTH AS THE SCOUT BEARS DOWN ON HIM AND OPENS FIRE WITH HIS LASER CANNON. LUKE IGNITES HIS LASER SWORD AND BEGINS DEFLECTING THE BOLTS. THE SCOUT'S BIKE KEEPS COMING AND IT APPEARS THAT IN A SECOND IT WILL CUT LUKE IN HALF. AT THE LAST INSTANT, LUKE STEPS ASIDE AND CHOPS OFF THE BIKE'S CONTROL VANES WITH ONE MIGHTY SLASH.

THE SCOUT'S BIKE
BEGINS TO PITCH AND
ROLL, THEN SLAMS
DIRECTLY INTO A TREE
IN A GIANT BALL OF
FIRE.

076

EXTERIOR SCOUT CAMPSITE – FOREST

HAN, CHEWIE AND THE DROIDS,
ALONG WITH THE REST OF THE
SQUAD, WAIT ANXIOUSLY IN THE
CLEARING. ARTOO'S RADAR SCREEN
STICKS OUT OF HIS DOMED HEAD
AND REVOLVES, SCANNING THE
FOREST. HE BEEPS.

THREEPIO

Oh, General Solo, somebody's coming.

HAN, CHEWIE, AND THE REST OF
THE SQUAD RAISE THEIR WEAPONS.

THREEPIO

Oh!

LUKE RUNS OUT OF THE FOLIAGE.

HAN

Luke! Where's Leia?

LUKE (CONCERNED)

What? She didn't come back?

HAN

I thought she was with you.

LUKE

We got separated.

LUKE AND HAN EXCHANGE A
SILENT, GRIM LOOK.

LUKE

Hey, we better go look for her.

HAN SIGNALS TO A REBEL
OFFICER.

HAN

Take the squad ahead. We'll meet at the shield
generator at 0300.

LUKE

Come on, Artoo. We'll need your scanners.

LUKE, CHEWIE, HAN AND THE DROIDS MOVE OFF IN ONE DIRECTION AS THE SQUAD PROCEEDS IN ANOTHER.

THREEPIO

Don't worry, Master Luke. We know what to do.

THEY MOVE OFF INTO THE WOODS.

THREEPIO (TO ARTOO)

And you said it was pretty here. Ugh!

EXTERIOR FOREST CLEARING – LEIA'S CRASH SITE

A STRANGE LITTLE FURRY CREATURE WITH HUGE BLACK EYES COMES SLOWLY INTO VIEW. THE CREATURE IS AN EWOK, BY THE NAME OF WICKET. HE SEEMS SOMEWHAT PUZZLED, AND PRODS LEIA WITH A SPEAR. THE STUBBY BALL OF FUZZ JUMPS BACK AND PRODS HER AGAIN.

LEIA

Cut it out!

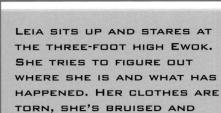

LEIA SITS UP AND STARES AT THE THREE-FOOT HIGH EWOK. SHE TRIES TO FIGURE OUT WHERE SHE IS AND WHAT HAS HAPPENED. HER CLOTHES ARE TORN, SHE'S BRUISED AND DISHEVELED.

THE EWOK HOLDS HIS FOUR-FOOT-LONG SPEAR IN A DEFENSIVE POSITION. LEIA STANDS UP, AND THE EWOK BACKS AWAY.

LEIA

I'm not gonna hurt you.

LEIA LOOKS AROUND AT THE DENSE FOREST, THEN SITS DOWN, WITH A SIGH, ON A FALLEN LOG.

LEIA

Well, looks like I'm stuck here. Trouble is, I don't know where here is. Maybe you can help me.

SHE LOOKS OVER AT THE WATCHFUL LITTLE EWOK AND PATS THE LOG BESIDE HER.

LEIA

Come on, sit down.

WICKET HOLDS HIS SPEAR UP WARILY AND GROWLS AT HER LIKE A PUPPY.

LEIA

I promise I won't hurt you. Now come here.

LEIA PATS THE LOG AGAIN, CAUSING MORE GROWLS AND SQUEAKS FROM THE LITTLE BEAR CREATURE.

LEIA

All right. You want something to eat?

SHE TAKES A SCRAP OF FOOD OUT OF HER POCKET AND OFFERS IT TO HIM. WICKET TAKES A STEP BACKWARD, THEN COCKS HIS HEAD AND MOVES CAUTIOUSLY TOWARD LEIA, CHATTERING IN HIS SQUEAKY EWOK LANGUAGE.

LEIA

That's right. Come on. Hmmm?

SNIFFING THE FOOD CAUTIOUSLY, THE EWOK COMES TOWARD LEIA AND SITS ON THE LOG BESIDE HER. SHE TAKES OFF HER HELMET, AND THE LITTLE CREATURE JUMPS BACK, STARTLED AGAIN. HE RUNS ALONG THE LOG, POINTING HIS SPEAR AT HER AND CHATTERING A BLUE STREAK. LEIA HOLDS OUT THE HELMET TO HIM.

LEIA

Look, it's a hat. It's not gonna hurt you. Look.

REASSURED, WICKET LOWERS HIS SPEAR AND CLIMBS BACK ON THE LOG, COMING TO INVESTIGATE THE HELMET.

LEIA

You're a jittery little thing, aren't you?

SUDDENLY, WICKET'S EARS PERK UP AND HE BEGINS TO SNIFF THE AIR. HE LOOKS AROUND WARILY, WHISPERING SOME EWOKESE WARNING TO LEIA.

LEIA

What is it?

Suddenly, a laser bolt comes out of the foliage and explodes on the log next to Leia. Leia and Wicket both roll backwards off the log, hiding behind it. Leia holds her own laser gun ready.

Another shot, and still no sight of anyone in the forest. Wicket disappears underneath the log. Suddenly a large Imperial scout is standing over her with his weapon pointed at her head. He reaches out his hand for her weapon.

SCOUT #1

Freeze! Come on, get up!

A second scout emerges from the foliage in front of the log.

SCOUT #1

Go get your ride and take her back to base.

SCOUT #2

Yes, sir.

The second scout starts toward his bike, as Wicket, crouched under the log, extends his spear and hits the first scout on the leg.

THE SCOUT JUMPS AND LETS OUT AN EXCLAMATION, AND LOOKS DOWN AT WICKET, PUZZLED. LEIA GRABS A BRANCH AND KNOCKS HIM OUT. SHE DIVES FOR HIS LASER PISTOL, AND THE SECOND SCOUT, NOW ON HIS BIKE, TAKES OFF. LEIA FIRES AWAY AND HITS THE ESCAPING BIKE, CAUSING IT TO CRASH INTO THE FIRST SCOUT'S BIKE, WHICH FLIES END OVER END AND EXPLODES. THE FOREST IS QUIET ONCE MORE. WICKET POKES HIS FUZZY HEAD UP FROM BEHIND THE LOG AND REGARDS LEIA WITH NEW RESPECT. HE MUMBLES HIS AWE. LEIA HURRIES OVER, LOOKING AROUND ALL THE TIME, AND MOTIONS THE CHUBBY LITTLE CREATURE INTO THE DENSE FOLIAGE.

LEIA

Come on, let's get out of here.

AS THEY MOVE INTO THE FOLIAGE, WICKET SHRIEKS AND TUGS AT LEIA TO FOLLOW HIM.

EXTERIOR DEATH STAR SURFACE

TIE FIGHTERS PATROL.

INTERIOR EMPEROR'S TOWER – THRONE ROOM

TWO RED IMPERIAL GUARDS STAND WATCH AT THE ELEVATOR AS THE DOOR OPENS TO REVEAL VADER. VADER ENTERS THE EERIE, FOREBODING THRONE ROOM. IT APPEARS TO BE EMPTY. HIS FOOTSTEPS ECHO AS HE APPROACHES THE THRONE. HE WAITS, ABSOLUTELY STILL. THE EMPEROR SITS WITH HIS BACK TO THE DARK LORD.

EMPEROR

I told you to remain on the command ship.

VADER

A small Rebel force has penetrated the shield and landed on Endor.

EMPEROR (NO SURPRISE)

Yes, I know.

VADER (AFTER A BEAT)

My son is with them.

EMPEROR (VERY COOL)

Are you sure?

VADER

I have felt him, my Master.

EMPEROR

Strange, that I have not. I wonder if your feelings on this matter are clear, Lord Vader.

VADER KNOWS WHAT IS BEING ASKED.

VADER

They are clear, my Master.

EMPEROR

Then you must go to the Sanctuary Moon and wait for him.

VADER (SKEPTICAL)

He will come to me?

EMPEROR

I have foreseen it. His compassion for you will be his undoing. He will come to you and then you will bring him before me.

VADER (BOWS)

As you wish.

THE DARK LORD STRIDES OUT OF THE THRONE ROOM.

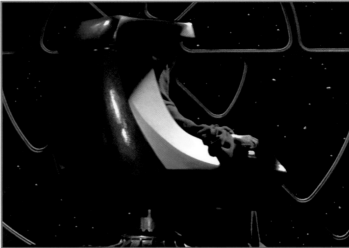

EXTERIOR FOREST CLEARING
– LEIA'S CRASH SITE

MOVING THROUGH THE HEAVY FOLIAGE NEAR
THE CLEARING WHERE WE LAST SAW LEIA,
LUKE FINDS LEIA'S HELMET, AND PICKS IT
UP WITH AN EXPRESSION OF CONCERN.

HAN (OFFSCREEN)

Luke! Luke!

LUKE RUNS WITH THE HELMET TO WHERE
HAN HAS FOUND THE CHARRED WRECKAGE
OF A SPEEDER BIKE IN THE GRASS.

THREEPIO

Oh, Master Luke.

LUKE

There's two more wrecked speeders back there. And I
found this.

HE TOSSES THE HELMET TO HAN.

THREEPIO

I'm afraid that Artoo's sensors can find no trace of Princess Leia.

HAN (GRAVELY)

I hope she's all right.

CHEWBACCA GROWLS, SNIFFING THE AIR, THEN, WITH A BARK, PUSHES OFF THROUGH THE FOLIAGE.

HAN

What, Chewie? What, Chewie?

THE OTHERS RUSH TO KEEP UP WITH THE GIANT WOOKIEE.

EXTERIOR FOREST – DENSE FOLIAGE

THE GROUP HAS REACHED A BREAK IN THE UNDERGROWTH. CHEWIE WALKS UP TO A TALL STAKE PLANTED IN THE GROUND. THERE IS A DEAD ANIMAL HANGING FROM IT.

HAN

Hey, I don't get it.

THE REST OF THE GROUP JOINS THE WOOKIEE AROUND THE STAKE.

HAN (CONTINUING)

Nah. It's just a dead animal, Chewie.

CHEWIE CAN'T RESIST. HE REACHES TOWARDS THE MEAT.

LUKE

Chewie, wa-wait! Don't!

TOO LATE. THE WOOKIEE HAS ALREADY PULLED THE ANIMAL FROM THE STAKE. SPROOING! THE GROUP FINDS ITSELF HANGING IN AN EWOK NET, SUSPENDED HIGH ABOVE THE CLEARING. CHEWIE HOWLS HIS REGRET. THEIR BODIES ARE A JUMBLE IN THE NET.

085

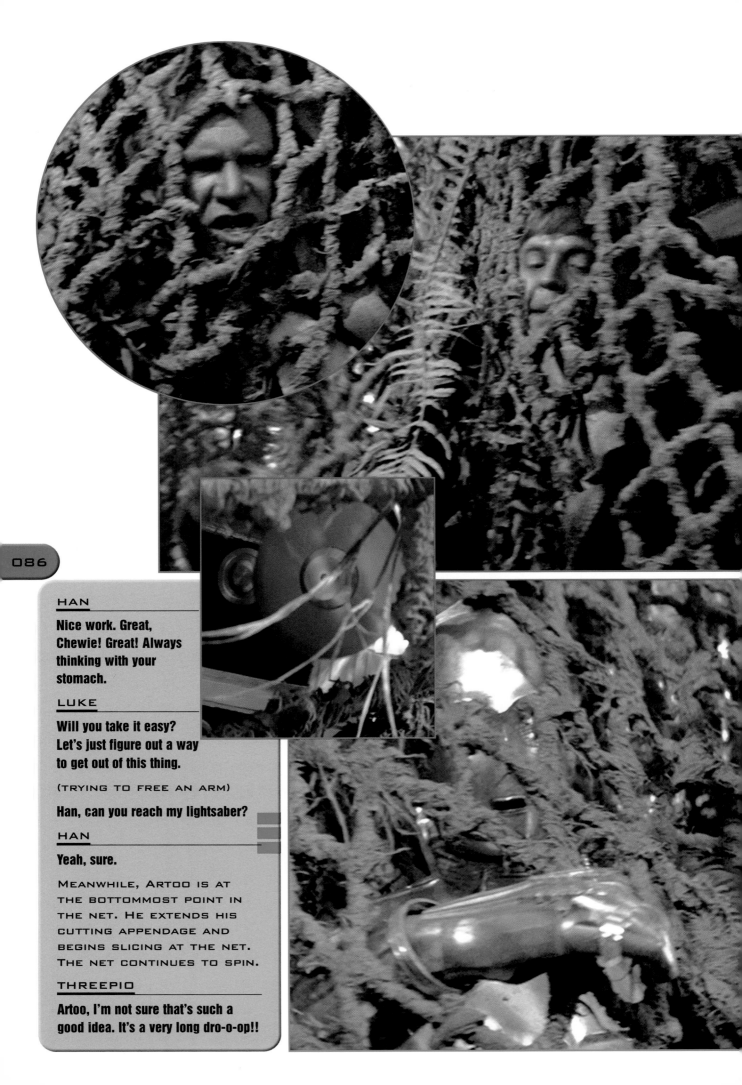

HAN

Nice work. Great, Chewie! Great! Always thinking with your stomach.

LUKE

Will you take it easy? Let's just figure out a way to get out of this thing.

(TRYING TO FREE AN ARM)

Han, can you reach my lightsaber?

HAN

Yeah, sure.

MEANWHILE, ARTOO IS AT THE BOTTOMMOST POINT IN THE NET. HE EXTENDS HIS CUTTING APPENDAGE AND BEGINS SLICING AT THE NET. THE NET CONTINUES TO SPIN.

THREEPIO

Artoo, I'm not sure that's such a good idea. It's a very long dro-o-op!!

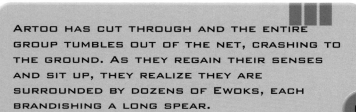

ARTOO HAS CUT THROUGH AND THE ENTIRE
GROUP TUMBLES OUT OF THE NET, CRASHING TO
THE GROUND. AS THEY REGAIN THEIR SENSES
AND SIT UP, THEY REALIZE THEY ARE
SURROUNDED BY DOZENS OF EWOKS, EACH
BRANDISHING A LONG SPEAR.

HAN

Wait...? Hey! Point that thing someplace else.

HAN PUSHES THE SPEAR WIELDED BY TEEBO OUT
OF HIS FACE AND A SECOND EWOK WARRIOR
COMES UP TO
ARGUE WITH TEEBO.
THE SPEAR
RETURNS TO HAN'S
FACE.

HAN

Hey!

HAN GRABS THE SPEAR ANGRILY AND STARTS TO GO FOR HIS LASER PISTOL.

LUKE

Han, don't. It'll be all right.

THE EWOKS SWARM THROUGH THEM AND CONFISCATE THEIR WEAPONS. LUKE GIVES THEM HIS LIGHTSABER.

LUKE

Chewie, give 'em your crossbow.

CHEWIE GROWLS AT THE FURRY CRITTERS. THREEPIO GETS FREE OF THE NET AND SITS UP, RATTLED.

THREEPIO

Oh, my head. Oh, my goodness!

WHEN THE EWOKS SEE THREEPIO, THEY LET OUT A GASP AND CHATTER AMONG THEMSELVES. THE EWOKS BEGIN TO CHANT AT THREEPIO, AND BOW DOWN BEFORE HIM. CHEWIE LETS OUT A PUZZLED BARK. HAN AND LUKE REGARD THE BOWED CREATURES IN WONDER. THREEPIO SPAEKS TO THEM IN THEIR NATIVE TONGUE.

LUKE

Do you understand anything they're saying?

THREEPIO

Oh, yes, Master Luke! Remember that I am fluent in over six million forms of communication.

HAN

What are you telling them?

THREEPIO

Hello, I think...I could be mistaken. They're using a very primitive dialect. But I do believe they think I am some sort of god.

THE OTHERS THINK THAT'S VERY FUNNY.

HAN

Well, why don't you use your divine influence and get us out of this?

THREEPIO

I beg your pardon, General Solo, but that just wouldn't be proper.

HAN

Proper?!

THREEPIO

It's against my programming to impersonate a deity.

089

HAN MOVES TOWARDS THREEPIO THREATENINGLY.

HAN

Why, you...

THE EWOKS MOVE IN TO PROTECT THEIR GOD AND HAN IS SURROUNDED BY A MENACING CIRCLE OF SPEARS, ALL AIMED AT HIM. HE HOLDS UP HIS HANDS PLACATINGLY.

HAN

My mistake. He's an old friend of mine.

EXTERIOR FOREST

A PROCESSION OF EWOKS WINDS THROUGH THE EVER-DARKENING FOREST. THEIR PRISONERS – HAN, LUKE, CHEWIE AND ARTOO – ARE TIED TO LONG POLES.

EACH POLE IS CARRIED ON THE SHOULDERS OF SEVERAL EWOKS.

EXTERIOR FOREST WALKWAY
– MOON FOREST

BEHIND THE CAPTIVES,
THREEPIO IS CARRIED ON A
LITTER, LIKE A KING, BY THE
REMAINING CREATURES.

THE PROCESSION MOVES
ALONG A SHAKY, NARROW,
WOODEN WALKWAY, HIGH IN
THE GIANT TREES. IT STOPS
AT THE END OF THE WALKWAY,
WHICH DROPS OFF INTO
NOTHINGNESS. ON THE OTHER
SIDE OF THE ABYSS IS A
VILLAGE OF MUD HUTS AND
RICKETY WALKWAYS, ATTACHED
TO THE GIANT TREES. THE
LEAD EWOK TAKES HOLD OF A
LONG VINE AND SWINGS
ACROSS TO THE VILLAGE
SQUARE; THE OTHER EWOKS
FOLLOW SUIT.

EXTERIOR EWOK VILLAGE SQUARE

THE PROCESSION WINDS ITS
WAY INTO THE VILLAGE
SQUARE. THE GROUP STOPS
BEFORE THE LARGEST HUT.

HAN, LUKE, CHEWIE, AND
ARTOO ARE STILL BOUND
TO THEIR POLES. HAN IS
PLACED ON A SPIT ABOVE
WHAT LOOKS LIKE A
BARBECUE PIT. THREEPIO'S
LITTER/THRONE IS GENTLY
PLACED NEAR THE PIT. HE
WATCHES WITH RAPT
FASCINATION. HAN, LUKE AND
CHEWIE ARE LESS
FASCINATED. CHEWIE GROWLS
HIS CONCERN.

HAN

I have a really bad feeling about this.

SUDDENLY, ALL ACTIVITY
STOPS AS LOGRAY, THE
TRIBAL MEDICINE MAN,
COMES OUT OF THE BIG HUT.
HE GOES TO THREEPIO,
WHOSE THRONE HAS BEEN
PLACED ON AN ELEVATED
PLATFORM. HE IS HOLDING
LUKE'S LIGHTSABER.

LOGRAY SPEAKS TO THREEPIO
AND THE ASSEMBLAGE OF
FUZZY EWOKS, POINTING TO
THE PRISONERS.

HAN

What did he say?

THREEPIO

I'm rather embarrassed, General Solo, but it appears you are to be the main course at a banquet in my honor.

THE EWOKS BEGIN FILLING THE PIT UNDER HAN WITH FIREWOOD.

THE DRUMS START BEATING, AND ALL THE FURRYHEADS TURN TO THE LARGE HUT. LEIA EMERGES, WEARING AN ANIMAL-SKIN DRESS. SHE SEES WHAT'S HAPPENING AT THE SAME MOMENT THE PRISONERS SEE HER.

LUKE

Leia?

HAN

Leia!

As she moves toward them, the Ewoks block her way with raised spears.

LEIA

Oh!

THREEPIO

Your Royal Highness.

Leia looks around at the assembled Ewoks and sighs.

LEIA

But these are my friends. Threepio, tell them they must be set free.

Threepio talks to Logray, who listens and shakes his head negatively. The Medicine Man gestures toward the prisoners and barks some orders.

Several Ewoks jump up and pile more wood on the barbecue with vigor.

HAN

Somehow, I got the feeling that didn't help us very much.

LUKE

Threepio, tell them if they don't do as you wish, you'll become angry and use your magic.

THREEPIO

But Master Luke, what magic? I couldn't possibly–

LUKE

Just tell them.

Threepio speaks to the Ewoks. The Ewoks are disturbed. Logray calls Threepio's bluff.

THREEPIO

You see, Master Luke, they didn't believe me. Just as I said they wouldn't.

Luke closes his eyes and begins to concentrate.

Now the litter/throne, with Threepio sitting upon it, rises from the ground. At first Threepio doesn't notice and keeps talking.

THREEPIO

Wha-wha-what's happening! Oh, dear! Oh!

The Ewoks fall back in terror from the floating throne. Now Threepio begins to spin as though he were on a revolving stool, with Threepio calling out in total panic at his situation.

THREEPIO

Put me down! He-e-elp! Somebody help! Master Luke! Artoo! Somebody, somebody, help! Master Luke, Artoo! Artoo, quickly! Do something, somebody! Oh! Ohhh!

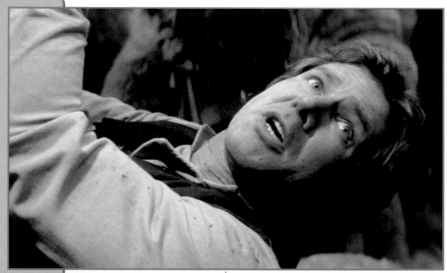

LOGRAY YELLS ORDERS TO THE COWERING
EWOKS. THEY RUSH UP AND RELEASE THE
BOUND PRISONERS. ARTOO CRASHES TO
THE GROUND. WHEN THE EWOKS SET HIM
UPRIGHT, THE LITTLE DROID IS FIGHTING
MAD. ARTOO BEEPS A BLUE STREAK AT THE
NEAREST EWOK AND BEGINS PURSUING HIM,
FINALLY GETTING CLOSE ENOUGH TO ZAP
HIM WITH AN ELECTRIC CHARGE. THE EWOK
JUMPS TWO FEET IN THE AIR AND RUNS
AWAY, SCREAMING. HAN ENFOLDS LEIA IN
AN EMBRACE. LUKE SLOWLY LOWERS
THREEPIO AND THE THRONE TO THE
GROUND.

THREEPIO

Oh, oh, oh, oh! Thank goodness.

LUKE

Thanks Threepio.

THREEPIO (STILL SHAKEN)

I...never knew I had it in me.

EXTERIOR FOREST WALKWAY

THE SOUNDS OF A COUNCIL CAN BE
HEARD.

EXTERIOR CHIEF'S HUT

YOUNGER EWOKS CRAM THE DOORWAY.

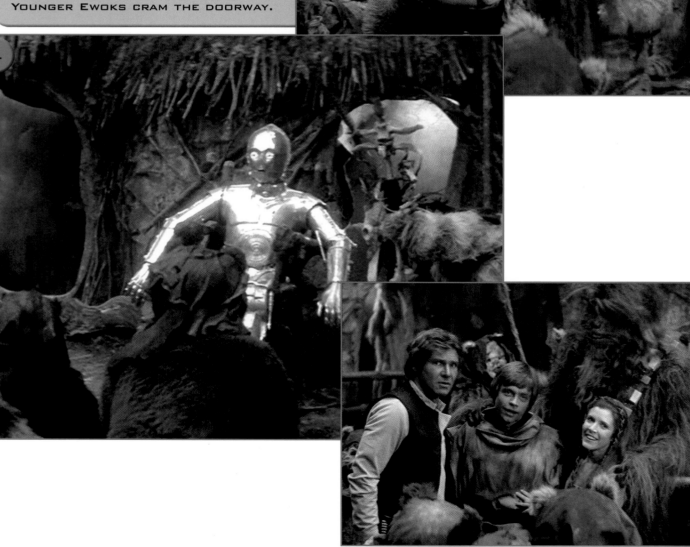

INTERIOR CHIEF'S HUT
– COUNCIL OF ELDERS

A GLOWING FIRE DANCES IN THE
CENTER OF THE SPARTAN, LOW-
CEILINGED ROOM, CREATING A
KALEIDOSCOPE OF SHADOWS ON THE
WALLS. ALONG ONE SIDE, A GROUP
OF TEN EWOK ELDERS FLANKS A
LARGER GRAY-HAIRED EWOK, CHIEF
CHIRPA, WHO SITS ON HIS THRONE.
THE REBELS SIT ALONG THE WALLS
OF THE HUT, WITH THREEPIO
BETWEEN THE TWO GROUPS AND
WICKET AND TEEBO OFF TO ONE
SIDE.

THREEPIO IS IN THE MIDST OF A
LONG, ANIMATED SPEECH IN THE
EWOKS' SQUEAKY NATIVE TONGUE.
THE EWOKS LISTEN CAREFULLY AND
OCCASIONALLY MURMUR COMMENTS
TO EACH OTHER.

THREEPIO POINTS SEVERAL TIMES AT
THE REBEL GROUP AND PANTOMIMES
A SHORT HISTORY OF THE GALACTIC
CIVIL WAR, MIMICKING THE
EXPLOSION AND ROCKET SOUNDS,
IMITATING IMPERIAL WALKERS.
THROUGHOUT THE LONG ACCOUNT,
CERTAIN FAMILIAR NAMES ARE
DISTINGUISHABLE IN ENGLISH:
PRINCESS LEIA, ARTOO, DARTH
VADER, DEATH STAR, JEDI, OBI-WAN
KENOBI. ARTOO BEGINS BEEPING
EXCITEDLY AT THREEPIO.

THREEPIO
_____

Yes, Artoo, I was just coming to that.

THREEPIO CONTINUES WITH:
MILLENNIUM FALCON, CLOUD CITY,
VADER, HAN SOLO, CARBONITE,
SARLACC, BRINGING THE HISTORY UP
TO THE PRESENT TIME.

AT THE END OF IT, THE CHIEF,
LOGRAY, AND THE ELDERS CONFER,
THEN NOD IN AGREEMENT.

HAN
_____

What's going on?

LEIA
_____

I don't know.

LUKE HAS BEEN SHARING THE JOY WITH
SMILING VISAGE, BUT NOW SOMETHING
PASSES LIKE A DARK CLOUD THROUGH HIS
CONSCIOUSNESS. THE OTHERS DO NOT
NOTICE.

LOGRAY MAKES A PRONOUNCEMENT.

THE DRUMS BEGIN TO SOUND, AND THE
EWOKS GESTICULATE WILDLY.

THREEPIO

Wonderful! We are now a part of the tribe.

SEVERAL OF THE LITTLE TEDDY BEARS RUN UP AND HUG THE REBELS.

HAN

Just what I always wanted.

LUKE WANDERS OUTSIDE INTO THE MOONLIGHT. LEIA NOTICES AND FOLLOWS.

CHEWBACCA IS BEING ENTHUSIASTICALLY EMBRACED BY AN EWOK, WHILE WICKET CLINGS TO HAN'S LEG.

HAN (CHUCKLES)

Well, short help is better than no help at all, Chewie.

(TO WICKET)

Thank you.

THREEPIO

He says the scouts are going to show us the quickest way to the shield generator.

HAN

Good. How far is it? Ask him. We need some fresh supplies, too. And try and get our weapons back.

HAN PULLS THREEPIO BACK AS HE KEEPS TRYING TO TRANSLATE.

HAN (CONTINUING)

And hurry up, will ya? I haven't got all day.

EXTERIOR EWOK VILLAGE

THE WALKWAY IS DESERTED NOW. THE
WINDOWS OF THE LITTLE HUTS GLOW AND
FLICKER FROM THE FIRES INSIDE. THE SOUNDS
OF THE FOREST FILL THE SOFT NIGHT AIR.
LUKE HAS WANDERED AWAY FROM THE
CHIEF'S HUT AND STANDS STARING UP AT THE
DEATH STAR. LEIA FINDS HIM LIKE THAT.

LEIA

Luke, what's wrong?

LUKE TURNS AND LOOKS AT HER A LONG
MOMENT.

LUKE

Leia...do you remember your mother? Your real
mother?

LEIA

Just a little bit. She died when I was very young.

LUKE

What do you remember?

LEIA

Just...images, really. Feelings.

LUKE

Tell me.

LEIA (A LITTLE SURPRISED
AT HIS INSISTENCE)

She was very beautiful. Kind, but...

(LOOKS UP)

sad. Why are you asking me this?

HE IS LOOKING AWAY.

LUKE

I have no memory of my mother. I never knew her.

LEIA

Luke, tell me. What's troubling you?

LUKE

Vader is here...now, on this moon.

LEIA (ALARMED)

How do you know?

LUKE

I felt his presence. He's come for me. He can feel
when I'm near. That's why I have to go.

(FACING HER)

As long as I stay, I'm endangering the group and our
mission here. I have to face him.

097

LEIA IS CONFUSED.

LEIA

Why?

LUKE

He's my father.

LEIA

Your father?!

LUKE

There's more. It won't be easy for you to hear it, but you must. If I don't make it back, you're the only hope for the Alliance.

LEIA IS VERY DISTURBED BY THIS.

LEIA

Luke, don't talk that way. You have a power I...I don't understand and could never have.

LUKE

You're wrong, Leia. You have that power too. In time, you'll learn to use it as I have. The Force is strong in my family. My father has it...I have it...and my sister has it.

LEIA STARES INTO HIS EYES. WHAT SHE SEES FRIGHTENS HER. BUT SHE DOESN'T DRAW AWAY. SHE BEGINS TO UNDERSTAND.

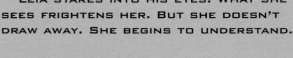

LUKE

Yes. It's you, Leia.

LEIA

I know. Somehow...I've always known.

LUKE

Then you know why I have to face him.

LEIA

No! Luke, run away, far away. If he can feel your presence, then leave this place. I wish I could go with you.

LUKE

No, you don't. You've always been strong.

LEIA

But why must you confront him?

LUKE

Because...there is good in him. I've felt it. He won't turn me over to the Emperor. I can save him. I can turn him back to the good side. I have to try.

THEY HOLD EACH OTHER AND LOOK AT EACH OTHER, BROTHER AND SISTER.

LEIA HOLDS BACK HER TEARS AS LUKE SLOWLY LETS HER GO AND MOVES AWAY. HE DISAPPEARS ON TO THE WALKWAY THAT LEADS OUT OF THE VILLAGE.

LEIA, BATHED IN MOONLIGHT, WATCHES HIM GO AS HAN COMES OUT OF THE CHIEF'S HUT AND COMES OVER TO HER.

HAN

Hey, what's goin' on?

LEIA

Nothing – I just want to be alone for a little while.

HAN (ANGRY)

Nothing? Come on, tell me. What's goin' on?

SHE LOOKS UP AT HIM, STRUGGLING TO CONTROL HERSELF.

LEIA

I…I can't tell you.

HAN (LOSES HIS TEMPER)

Could you tell Luke? Is that who you could tell?

LEIA

I…

HAN

Ahhh…

HE STARTS TO WALK AWAY, EXASPERATED, THEN STOPS AND WALKS BACK TO HER.

HAN

I'm sorry.

LEIA

Hold me.

HAN GATHERS HER TIGHTLY IN HIS PROTECTIVE EMBRACE.

EXTERIOR FOREST – IMPERIAL LANDING PLATFORM

AN IMPERIAL SHUTTLE FLOATS DOWN FROM THE DEATH STAR AND LANDS GRACEFULLY ON THE HUGE PLATFORM.

NOW, AN IMPERIAL WALKER APPROACHES THE PLATFORM FROM THE DARKNESS OF THE FOREST. THE WHOLE OUTPOST – PLATFORM, WALKERS, MILITARY – LOOKS PARTICULARLY OFFENSIVE IN THE MIDST OF THIS VERDANT BEAUTY.

EXTERIOR IMPERIAL LANDING
PLATFORM – LOWER DECK

DARTH VADER WALKS DOWN THE RAMP OF
THE SHUTTLE ON TO THE PLATFORM.
COMING OUT OF AN ELEVATOR, HE APPEARS
ON A RAMP ON A LOWER LEVEL. HE WALKS
TOWARD ANOTHER RAMP EXIT AND IS MET BY
TWO TROOPERS AND A COMMANDER WITH
LUKE, IN BINDERS, AT THEIR CENTER. THE
YOUNG JEDI GAZES AT VADER WITH
COMPLETE CALM.

COMMANDER

This is a Rebel that surrendered to us.
Although he denies it, I believe there may
be more of them, and I request permission
to conduct a further search of the area.

VADER LOOKS AT LUKE, TURNS
AWAY AND FACES THE
COMMANDER.

COMMANDER

He was armed only with this.

THE COMMANDER PLACES LUKE'S
LIGHTSABER IN VADER'S HANDS.

VADER

Good work, Commander. Leave us.
Conduct your search and bring his
    companions to me.

COMMANDER

Yes, my lord.

THE OFFICER AND TROOPS
WITHDRAW. VADER AND LUKE ARE
LEFT ALONE ON THE RAMP.

VADER

The Emperor has been expecting you.

LUKE

I know, Father.

VADER

So, you have accepted the truth.

LUKE

I've accepted the truth that you were once Anakin
Skywalker, my Father.

VADER (TURNING TO FACE HIM)

That name no longer has any meaning for me.

LUKE

It is the name of your true self. You've only forgotten. I
know there is good in you. The Emperor hasn't driven
it from you fully. That was why you couldn't destroy
me. That's why you won't bring me to your Emperor
now.

VADER LOOKS DOWN FROM
LUKE TO THE LIGHTSABER IN
HIS OWN BLACK-GLOVED HAND.
HE SEEMS TO PONDER LUKE'S
WORDS.

VADER IGNITES THE LIGHTSABER
AND HOLDS IT TO EXAMINE ITS
HUMMING, BRILLIANT BLADE.

VADER

I see you have constructed a new
lightsaber. Your skills are complete.

(EXTINGUISHING THE
LIGHTSABER)

Indeed, you are powerful, as the Emperor has
foreseen.

LUKE

Come with me.

VADER

Obi-Wan once thought as you do. You don't know the
power of the dark side. I must obey my master.

LUKE

I will not turn...and you'll be forced to kill me.

VADER

If that is your
destiny...

LUKE

Search your feelings,
Father. You can't do
this. I feel the conflict
within you. Let go of
your hate.

VADER

It is too late for me,
son.

(SIGNALING TO
SOME DISTANT
STORMTROOPERS)

The Emperor will show
you the true nature of
the Force. He is your
master now.

VADER AND LUKE
STAND STARING AT
ONE ANOTHER FOR
A LONG MOMENT.

LUKE

Then my father is truly dead.

HAN, LEIA, CHEWBACCA, THE DROIDS,
WICKET AND ANOTHER EWOK SCOUT,
PAPLOO, HIDE ON A RIDGE OVERLOOKING
THE MASSIVE IMPERIAL SHIELD GENERATOR.

AT THE BASE OF THE GENERATOR IS AN
IMPERIAL LANDING PLATFORM. LEIA STUDIES
THE INSTALLATION.

LEIA

The main entrance to the control bunker's on the far
side of that landing platform. This isn't going to be
easy.

HAN

Hey, don't worry. Chewie and me got into a lot of
places more heavily guarded than this.

WICKET AND PAPLOO ARE CHATTERING AWAY
IN EWOK LANGUAGE. THEY SPEAK TO
THREEPIO.

LEIA

What's he saying?

THREEPIO

He says there's a secret entrance on the other side of
the ridge.

EXTERIOR SPACE — REBEL FLEET

THE VAST FLEET HANGS IN SPACE. A
GIANT REBEL STAR CRUISER IS UP AT
THE FRONT, BUT NOW THE MILLENNIUM
FALCON ROARS UP TO A SPOT AHEAD OF IT,
TINY IN COMPARISON.

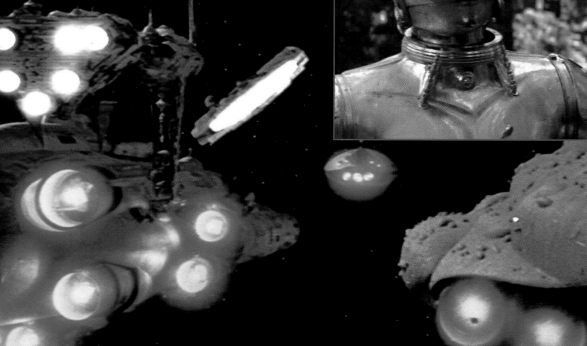

INTERIOR MILLENNIUM FALCON – COCKPIT

LANDO IS IN THE PILOT SEAT.

LANDO

Admiral, we're in position. All fighters accounted for.

INTERIOR REBEL STAR CRUISER – BRIDGE

ACKBAR

Proceed with the countdown. All groups assume attack coordinates.

INTERIOR MILLENNIUM FALCON – COCKPIT

LANDO'S ALIEN COPILOT, NIEN NUNB, TAKES SOME GETTING USED TO IN THE FAMILIAR ENVIRONS OF THE FALCON'S COCKPIT. LANDO TURNS TO HIS WEIRD COPILOT.

LANDO

Don't worry, my friend's down there. He'll have that shield down on time...

THE COPILOT FLIPS SOME SWITCHES AND GRUNTS AN ALIEN COMMENT.

LANDO (TO HIMSELF)

...or this'll be the shortest offensive of all time.

INTERIOR REBEL STAR CRUISER – BRIDGE

ACKBAR

All craft, prepare to jump into hyperspace on my mark.

INTERIOR MILLENNIUM FALCON – COCKPIT

LANDO

All right. Stand by.

HE PULLS A LEVER, AND THE STARS OUTSIDE BEGIN TO STREAK.

EXTERIOR SPACE – REBEL FLEET

WE ARE TREATED TO AN AWESOME SIGHT: FIRST THE MILLENNIUM FALCON, THEN ACKBAR'S STAR CRUISER, THEN, IN LARGE SEGMENTS, THE HUGE FLEET ROAR INTO HYPERSPACE.

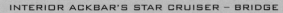

INTERIOR ACKBAR'S STAR CRUISER – BRIDGE

THE STARS STREAK BY ACKBAR ON HIS BRIDGE.

EXTERIOR SPACE – REBEL FLEET

THE REMAINDER OF THE REBEL FLEET ROARS INTO HYPERSPACE. AND DISAPPEARS.

EXTERIOR ENDOR – RIDGE OVERLOOKING CONTROL BUNKER

HAN, LEIA, CHEWIE, THE DROIDS AND THEIR TWO EWOK GUIDES, WICKET AND PAPLOO, HAVE REUNITED WITH THE REBEL STRIKE SQUAD. THE ENTIRE GROUP IS SPREAD THROUGH THE THICK UNDERGROWTH. BENEATH THEM IS THE BUNKER THAT LEADS INTO THE GENERATOR. FOUR IMPERIAL SCOUTS, THEIR SPEEDER BIKES PARKED NEAR BY, KEEP WATCH OVER THE BUNKER ENTRANCE. PAPLOO CHATTERS AWAY TO HAN IN EWOK LANGUAGE.

HAN

Back door, huh? Good idea.

WICKET AND PAPLOO CONTINUE THEIR EWOK CONVERSATION.

HAN (CONTINUING)

It's only a few guards. This shouldn't be too much trouble.

LEIA

Well, it only takes one to sound the alarm.

HAN (WITH SELF-CONFIDENT GRIN)

Then we'll do it real quiet-like.

PAPLOO HAS SCAMPERED INTO THE UNDERBRUSH. THREEPIO ASKS WICKET WHERE PAPLOO WENT AND IS GIVEN A SHORT REPLY.

THREEPIO

Oh! Oh, my. Uh, Princess Leia!

LEIA QUIETS HIM.

THREEPIO

I'm afraid our furry companion has gone and done something rather rash.

CHEWIE BARKS. HAN, LEIA AND COMPANY WATCH IN DISTRESS.

LEIA

Oh, no.

EXTERIOR THE BUNKER ENTRANCE

PAPLOO HAS SLIPPED OUT OF THE UNDERGROWTH NEAR WHERE THE IMPERIAL SCOUTS ARE LOUNGING.

HAN (SIGHS)

There goes our surprise attack.

PAPLOO SILENTLY SWINGS HIS FURRY BALL OF A BODY ONTO ONE OF THE SCOUTS' SPEEDER BIKES AND BEGINS FLIPPING SWITCHES AT RANDOM. SUDDENLY, THE BIKE'S ENGINE FIRES UP WITH A TREMENDOUS ROAR.

EXTERIOR RIDGE

HAN, LEIA AND COMPANY WATCH IN DISTRESS.

SCOUT

Look! Over there! Stop him!

THE IMPERIAL SCOUTS RACE TOWARD PAPLOO JUST AS HIS SPEEDER BIKE COMES INTO MOTION. PAPLOO HANGS ON BY HIS PAWS AND SHOOTS AWAY INTO THE FOREST.

THREE OF THE IMPERIAL SCOUTS JUMP ON THEIR ROCKET BIKES AND SPEED AWAY IN PURSUIT. THE FOURTH WATCHES THEM GO.

EXTERIOR RIDGE

HAN, LEIA, AND CHEWIE EXCHANGE DELIGHTED LOOKS.

HAN

Not bad for a little furball. There's only one left.

(TO WICKET)

You stay here. We'll take care of this.

Threepio moves to stand next to Wicket and Artoo.

THREEPIO

I have decided that we shall stay here.

EXTERIOR FOREST

Paploo sails through the trees, more lucky than in control. It's scary, but he loves it. When the Imperial scouts pull within sight behind him and begin firing laser bolts, he decides he's had enough. As he rounds a tree, out of their sight, Paploo grabs a vine and swings up into the trees. A moment later, the scouts tear under him in pursuit of the still-flying, unoccupied bike.

EXTERIOR BUNKER

Han sneaks up behind the remaining Imperial scout, taps him on the shoulder and lets the scout chase him behind the bunker into the arms of the waiting Rebel strike team.

INTERIOR BUNKER

The group enters the bunker silently.

EXTERIOR SPACE – DEATH STAR

THE HALF-COMPLETED DEATH STAR HANGS IN SPACE OVER THE MOON OF ENDOR.

INTERIOR DEATH STAR
– EMPEROR'S THRONE ROOM

THE ELEVATOR OPENS. VADER AND LUKE ENTER THE ROOM ALONE. THEY WALK ACROSS THE DARK SPACE TO STAND BEFORE THE THRONE, FATHER AND SON, SIDE BY SIDE BENEATH THE GAZE OF THE EMPEROR. VADER BOWS TO HIS MASTER.

EMPEROR

Welcome, young Skywalker. I have been expecting you.

LUKE PEERS AT THE HOODED FIGURE DEFIANTLY. THE EMPEROR SMILES, THEN LOOKS DOWN AT LUKE'S BINDERS.

EMPEROR

You no longer need those.

THE EMPEROR MOTIONS EVER SO SLIGHTLY WITH HIS FINGER AND LUKE'S BINDERS FALL AWAY, CLATTERING NOISILY TO THE FLOOR. LUKE LOOKS DOWN AT HIS OWN HANDS, FREE NOW TO REACH OUT AND GRAB THE EMPEROR'S NECK. HE DOES NOTHING.

EMPEROR

Guards, leave us.

THE RED-CLOAKED GUARDS TURN AND DISAPPEAR BEHIND THE ELEVATOR.

EMPEROR
(TO LUKE)

I'm looking forward to completing your training. In time you will call me Master.

LUKE

You're gravely mistaken. You won't convert me as you did my father.

THE EMPEROR GETS DOWN FROM HIS THRONE AND WALKS UP VERY CLOSE TO LUKE. THE EMPEROR LOOKS INTO HIS EYES AND, FOR THE FIRST TIME, LUKE CAN PERCEIVE THE EVIL VISAGE WITHIN THE HOOD.

EMPEROR

Oh, no, my young Jedi. You will find that it is you who are mistaken...about a great many things.

VADER

His lightsaber.

VADER EXTENDS A GLOVED HAND TOWARD THE EMPEROR, REVEALING LUKE'S LIGHTSABER. THE EMPEROR TAKES IT.

EMPEROR

Ah, yes, a Jedi's weapon. Much like your father's. By now you must know your father can never be turned from the dark side. So will it be with you.

LUKE

You're wrong. Soon I'll be dead...and you with me.

THE EMPEROR LAUGHS.

EMPEROR

Perhaps you refer to the imminent attack of your Rebel fleet.

LUKE LOOKS DOWN MOMENTARILY.

EMPEROR

Yes...I assure you we are quite safe from your friends here.

LUKE

Your overconfidence is your weakness.

VADER LOOKS AT LUKE.

EMPEROR

Your faith in your friends is yours.

VADER

It is pointless to resist, my son.

THE EMPEROR HAS RETURNED TO HIS THRONE AND NOW TURNS TO FACE LUKE.

EMPEROR (ANGRY)

Everything that has transpired has done so according to my design. Your friends

(INDICATES ENDOR)

up there on the Sanctuary Moon...

LUKE REACTS.

EMPEROR (CONTINUING)

...are walking into a trap. As is your Rebel fleet! It was I who allowed the Alliance to know the location of the shield generator. It is quite safe from your pitiful little band. An entire legion of my best troops awaits them.

LUKE'S LOOK DARTS FROM THE EMPEROR TO THE SWORD IN THE EMPEROR'S HAND.

EMPEROR

Oh...I'm afraid the deflector shield will be quite operational when your friends arrive.

INTERIOR BUNKER – MAIN CONTROL ROOM

HAN, LEIA, CHEWIE AND THE REBEL STRIKE TEAM STORM THROUGH A DOOR AND ENTER THE MAIN CONTROL ROOM, TAKING ALL OF THE PERSONNEL PRISONER.

HAN

All right! Up! Move! Come on! Quickly! Quickly, Chewie.

THE REBEL TROOPS HERD THE GENERATOR CONTROLLERS AWAY FROM THEIR PANELS. LEIA GLANCES AT ONE OF THE SCREENS ON THE CONTROL PANEL.

LEIA

Han! Hurry! The fleet will be here any moment.

HAN

Charges! Come on, come on!

EXTERIOR BUNKER

SEVERAL MORE CONTROLLERS AND STORMTROOPERS RUN INTO THE BUNKER, LEAVING GUARDS AT THE DOOR. THREEPIO WATCHES NERVOUSLY IN THE BUSHES.

THREEPIO

Oh, my! They'll be captured!

WICKET CHATTERS IN EWOK LANGUAGE, AND THEN TAKES OFF FULL STEAM INTO THE FOREST.

THREEPIO

Wa-ait! Wait, come back! Artoo, stay with me.

INTERIOR BUNKER

IMPERIAL OFFICER

Freeze!

HAN LOOKS UP FROM SETTING CHARGES AS AN IMPERIAL OFFICER ENTERS. HE DEALS WITH HIM, BUT HE AND LEIA SPIN TO FIND DOZENS OF IMPERIAL WEAPONS TRAINED ON THEM AND THEIR COHORTS.

COMMANDER

You Rebel scum.

A POISED FORCE OF IMPERIAL TROOPS SURROUND THEM. EVEN MORE POUR INTO THE ROOM, ROUGHLY DISARMING THE REBEL CONTINGENT. HAN, LEIA, AND CHEWIE EXCHANGE LOOKS. THEY'RE HELPLESS.

INTERIOR MILLENNIUM FALCON – COCKPIT

LANDO OPERATES THE CONTROLS TO COME OUT OF HYPERSPACE.

EXTERIOR SPACE – ENDOR,
DEATH STAR, REBEL FLEET

THE REBEL FLEET COMES OUT OF HYPERSPACE WITH AN AWESOME ROAR. THE MILLENNIUM FALCON AND SEVERAL REBEL FIGHTERS ARE AT THE FRONT AS THE SPACE ARMADA BEARS DOWN ON ITS TARGET, THE DEATH STAR AND ITS SANCTUARY MOON.

INTERIOR REBEL STAR CRUISER – BRIDGE

ACKBAR SURVEYS HIS REBEL FLEET FROM THE BRIDGE.

INTERIOR MILLENNIUM FALCON – COCKPIT

LANDO FLIPS SWITCHES, CHECKS HIS SCREEN, AND SPEAKS INTO THE RADIO.

LANDO

All wings report in.

INTERIOR WEDGE'S X-FIGHTER – COCKPIT

WEDGE

Red Leader standing by.

INTERIOR GRAY LEADER'S
X-FIGHTER – COCKPIT

GRAY LEADER

Gray Leader standing by.

INTERIOR GREEN LEADER'S
X-FIGHTER – COCKPIT

GREEN LEADER

Green Leader standing by.

INTERIOR WEDGE'S X-FIGHTER – COCKPIT

WEDGE

Lock S-foils in attack positions.

EXTERIOR SPACE – REBEL FLEET

THE REBEL FLEET CONVERGES ON THE DEATH STAR.

INTERIOR REBEL STAR CRUISER

FROM THE BRIDGE OF THE REBEL HEADQUARTERS FRIGATE, ADMIRAL ACKBAR WATCHES THE FIGHTERS MASSING OUTSIDE HIS VIEWSCREEN.

ACKBAR

May the Force be with us.

INTERIOR MILLENNIUM FALCON – COCKPIT

LANDO LOOKS WORRIEDLY AT HIS ALIEN COPILOT, NIEN NUNB, WHO POINTS TO THE CONTROL PANEL AND TALKS TO LANDO.

LANDO

We've got to be able to get some kind of a reading on that shield, up or down. Well, how could they be jamming us if they don't know...we're coming?

LANDO SHOOTS A CONCERNED LOOK OUT AT THE APPROACHING DEATH STAR AS THE IMPLICATIONS OF WHAT HE'S JUST SAID SINK IN. HE HITS A SWITCH ON HIS COMLINK.

LANDO

Break off the attack! The shield is still up.

INTERIOR WEDGE'S X-FIGHTER – COCKPIT

WEDGE

I get no reading. Are you sure?

LANDO (VOICE-OVER)

Pull up!

INTERIOR MILLENNIUM FALCON – COCKPIT

LANDO

All craft pull up!

EXTERIOR SPACE – DEATH STAR SHIELD

THE FALCON AND THE FIGHTERS OF RED SQUAD VEER OFF DESPERATELY TO AVOID THE UNSEEN WALL.

INTERIOR REBEL STAR CRUISER – BRIDGE

ALARMS ARE SCREAMING AND LIGHTS FLASHING AS THE HUGE SHIP CHANGES COURSE ABRUPTLY. OTHER SHIPS IN THE FLEET SHOOT BY OUTSIDE AS THE ARMADA TRIES TO HALT ITS FORWARD MOMENTUM.

ACKBAR

Take evasive action! Green Group, stick close to holding sector MV-7.

EXTERIOR SPACE – DEATH STAR SHIELD

THE REBEL FLEET TAKES EVASIVE ACTION.

INTERIOR REBEL STAR CRUISER – BRIDGE

A MON CALAMARI CONTROLLER TURNS AWAY FROM HIS SCREEN AND CALLS OUT TO ACKBAR, QUITE EXCITED.

CONTROLLER

Admiral, we have enemy ships in sector 47.

THE ADMIRAL TURNS TO THE CONTROLLER.

ACKBAR

It's a trap!

EXTERIOR SPACE – REBEL FLEET

THE MILLENNIUM FALCON FLIES INTO THE IMPERIAL TRAP.

INTERIOR MILLENNIUM FALCON – COCKPIT

LANDO (OVER COMLINK)

Fighters coming in.

EXTERIOR SPACE

THE MILLENNIUM FALCON AND SEVERAL SQUADS OF REBEL FIGHTERS HEAD INTO AN ARMADA OF TIE FIGHTERS. THE SKY EXPLODES AS A FIERCE DOGFIGHT ENSUES IN AND AROUND THE GIANT REBEL CRUISERS.

INTERIOR REBEL COCKPIT

REBEL PILOT

There's too many of them!

EXTERIOR SPACE

THE MILLENNIUM FALCON FLIES THROUGH THE DOGFIGHT.

INTERIOR MILLENNIUM FALCON – COCKPIT

LANDO

Accelerate to attack speed! Draw their fire away from the cruisers.

INTERIOR WEDGE'S X-FIGHTER – COCKPIT

WEDGE

Copy, Gold Leader.

EXTERIOR SPACE – REBEL CRUISER

THE BATTLE CONTINUES AROUND THE GIANT CRUISERS.

112

INTERIOR DEATH STAR –
EMPEROR'S THRONE ROOM

THROUGH THE ROUND WINDOW
BEHIND THE EMPEROR'S
THRONE CAN BE SEEN THE
DISTANT FLASHES OF THE
SPACE BATTLE IN PROGRESS.

EMPEROR

Come, boy. See for yourself.

THE EMPEROR IS SITTING IN
HIS THRONE. LUKE MOVES TO
LOOK THROUGH A SMALL
SECTION OF THE WINDOW.
VADER ALSO MOVES FORWARD.

EMPEROR

From here you will witness the final
destruction of the Alliance, and the
end of your insignificant Rebellion.

LUKE IS IN TORMENT. HE
GLANCES AT HIS LIGHTSABER
SITTING ON THE ARMREST OF
THE THRONE. THE EMPEROR WATCHES HIM
AND SMILES, TOUCHES HIS LIGHTSABER.

EMPEROR

You want this, don't you? The hate is swelling in you
now. Take your Jedi weapon. Use it. I am unarmed.
Strike me down with it. Give in to your anger. With
each passing moment, you make yourself more my
servant.

VADER WATCHES LUKE IN HIS AGONY.

LUKE

No!

EMPEROR

It is unavoidable. It is your destiny. You, like your father, are now mine!

EXTERIOR FOREST
– GENERATOR BUNKER

HAN, LEIA, CHEWIE AND THE REST OF THE STRIKE TEAM ARE LED OUT OF THE BUNKER BY THEIR CAPTORS. THE SURROUNDING AREA, DESERTED BEFORE, IS NOW CROWDED WITH TWO-LEGGED IMPERIAL WALKERS AND HUNDREDS OF IMPERIAL TROOPS. THE SITUATION LOOKS HOPELESS.

STORMTROOPER

All right, move it! I said move it! Go on!

FROM THE UNDERGROWTH BEYOND THE CLEARING COMES THREEPIO.

THREEPIO

Hello! I say, over there! Were you looking for me?

BUNKER COMMANDER

Bring those two down here!

STORMTROOPER

Let's go.

ARTOO AND THREEPIO ARE STANDING
NEAR ONE OF THE BIG TREES. AS
SIX IMPERIAL STORMTROOPERS RUSH
OVER TO TAKE THEM CAPTIVE, THE
TWO DROIDS DUCK OUT OF SIGHT
BEHIND THE TREE.

THREEPIO

Well, they're on their way. Artoo, are you
sure this was a good idea?

STORMTROOPER

Freeze! Don't move!

THREEPIO

We surrender.

THE STORMTROOPERS COME AROUND
THE TREE AND FIND THE TWO
DROIDS WAITING QUIETLY TO BE
TAKEN. AS THE IMPERIAL TROOPS
MOVE TO DO THAT, HOWEVER, A
BAND OF EWOKS DROPS DOWN FROM
ABOVE AND OVERPOWERS THEM.

THREEPIO

Ohhh! Stand back, Artoo.

IN A NEARBY TREE, AN EWOK RAISES
A HORN TO HIS LIPS AND SOUNDS
THE EWOK ATTACK CALL.

All hell breaks loose as hundreds of Ewoks throw their fuzzy bodies into the fray against the assembled stormtroopers and their awesome two-legged walkers.

Stormtroopers fire on Ewoks with sophisticated weapons while their furry little adversaries sneak up behind the Imperial troopers and bash them over the head with large clubs.

Ewoks in handmade, primitive hanggliders drop rocks on to the stormtroopers, dive-bombing their deadly adversaries. One is hit in the wing with laser fire and crashes.

A line of Ewoks hangs desperately to a vine that is hooked to a walker's foot. As the walker moves along, the fuzzy creatures are dragged behind.

In the confusion of the battle, Han and Leia break away and dive for the cover of the bunker door as explosions erupt around them. Han goes to the bunker door control panel.

LEIA

The code's changed. We need Artoo!

HAN

Here's the terminal.

LEIA (INTO COMLINK)

Artoo, where are you? We need you at the bunker right away.

ARTOO AND THREEPIO ARE HIDING BEHIND A LOG AS THE BATTLE RAGES AROUND THEM. SUDDENLY, THE STUBBY LITTLE ASTRODROID LETS OUT A SERIES OF WHISTLES AND SHOOTS OFF ACROSS THE BATTLEFIELD. THREEPIO, PANICKED, RUNS AFTER HIM.

THREEPIO

Going? What do you mean, you're going? But – but going where, Artoo? No, wait! Artoo! Oh, this is no time for heroics. Come back!

A GROUP OF EWOKS HAS MOVED A PRIMITIVE CATAPULT INTO POSITION. THEY FIRE OFF A LARGE BOULDER THAT HITS ONE OF THE WALKERS. THE WALKER TURNS AND HEADS FOR THE CATAPULT, BLASTING AWAY WITH BOTH GUNS. THE EWOKS ABANDON THEIR WEAPONS AND FLEE IN ALL DIRECTIONS.

EXTERIOR OUTER SPACE

THE FALCON AND OTHER REBEL FIGHTERS
ARE ENGAGED IN A FEROCIOUS COMBAT WITH
IMPERIAL TIE FIGHTERS, THE BATTLE RAGING
AROUND THE CRUISERS OF THE REBEL
ARMADA.

INTERIOR MILLENNIUM FALCON – COCKPIT

LANDO IS IN RADIO COMMUNICATION WITH
THE PILOTS OF THE OTHER REBEL SQUADS.

LANDO

Watch yourself, Wedge! Three from above!

INTERIOR WEDGE'S X-FIGHTER – COCKPIT

WEDGE (OVER COMLINK)

Red Three, Red Two, pull in!

INTERIOR RED TWO'S X-FIGHTER – COCKPIT

RED TWO

Got it!

EXTERIOR SPACE

THE DOGFIGHT BETWEEN REBEL X-WINGS
AND IMPERIAL TIE FIGHTERS RAGES.

INTERIOR RED THREE'S X-FIGHTER – COCKPIT

RED THREE

Three of them coming in, twenty degrees!

INTERIOR WEDGE'S X-FIGHTER – COCKPIT

WEDGE

Cut to the left! I'll take the leader!

EXTERIOR SPACE

WEDGE SHOOTS DOWN THE TIE FIGHTER.

INTERIOR WEDGE'S X-FIGHTER – COCKPIT

WEDGE

**They're heading for
the medical frigate.**

EXTERIOR SPACE

LANDO STEERS THE FALCON THROUGH A COMPLETE FLIP, AS HIS CREW FIRES AT THE TIES FROM THE BELLY GUNS.

INTERIOR MILLENNIUM FALCON – COCKPIT

NAVIGATOR

Pressure steady.

EXTERIOR SPACE

THE COPILOT NIEN NUNB CHATTERS AN OBSERVATION.

THE GIANT IMPERIAL STAR DESTROYER WAITS SILENTLY SOME DISTANCE FROM THE BATTLE. THE EMPEROR'S HUGE SUPER STAR DESTROYER RESTS IN THE MIDDLE OF THE FLEET.

INTERIOR MILLENNIUM FALCON – COCKPIT

LANDO

Only the fighters are attacking...I wonder what those Star Destroyers are waiting for.

INTERIOR SUPER STAR DESTROYER

ADMIRAL PIETT AND TWO FLEET COMMANDERS WATCH THE BATTLE AT THE HUGE WINDOW OF THE SUPER STAR DESTROYER'S BRIDGE.

COMMANDER

We're in attack position now, sir.

PIETT

Hold here.

COMMANDER

We're not going to attack?

PIETT

I have my orders from the Emperor himself. He has something special planned. We only need to keep them from escaping.

INTERIOR EMPEROR'S TOWER – THRONE ROOM

A WORRIED LUKE WATCHES THE AERIAL BATTLE FIREWORKS OUT THE WINDOW AS REBEL SHIPS EXPLODE AGAINST THE PROTECTIVE SHIELD.

EMPEROR

As you can see, my young apprentice, your friends have failed. Now witness the firepower of this fully armed and operational battle station.

(INTO COMLINK)

Fire at will, Commander.

LUKE, IN SHOCK, LOOKS OUT TO THE REBEL FLEET BEYOND.

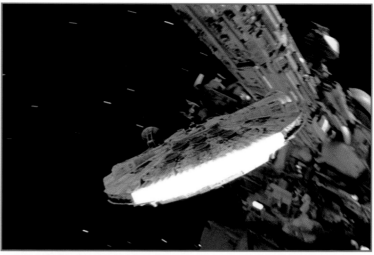

INTERIOR DEATH STAR – CONTROL ROOM

A BUTTON IS PRESSED, WHICH SWITCHES ON A PANEL OF LIGHTS. CONTROLLERS PULL BACK ON SEVERAL SWITCHES. A HOODED IMPERIAL SOLDIER REACHES OVERHEAD AND PULLS A LEVER. COMMANDER JERJERROD STANDS OVER THEM.

JERJERROD

Fire!

INTERIOR DEATH STAR – BLAST CHAMBER

A HUGE BEAM OF LIGHT EMANATES FROM A LONG SHAFT.

TWO STORMTROOPERS STAND TO ONE SIDE AT A CONTROL PANEL.

EXTERIOR DEATH STAR

THE GIANT LASER DISH ON THE COMPLETED HALF OF THE DEATH STAR BEGINS TO GLOW. THEN A POWERFUL BEAM SHOOTS OUT TOWARD THE AERIAL BATTLE.

120

EXTERIOR SPACE – AIR BATTLE

THE AIR IS THICK WITH GIANT SHIPS. NOW AN ENORMOUS REBEL CRUISER IS HIT BY THE DEATH STAR BEAM AND BLOWN TO DUST.

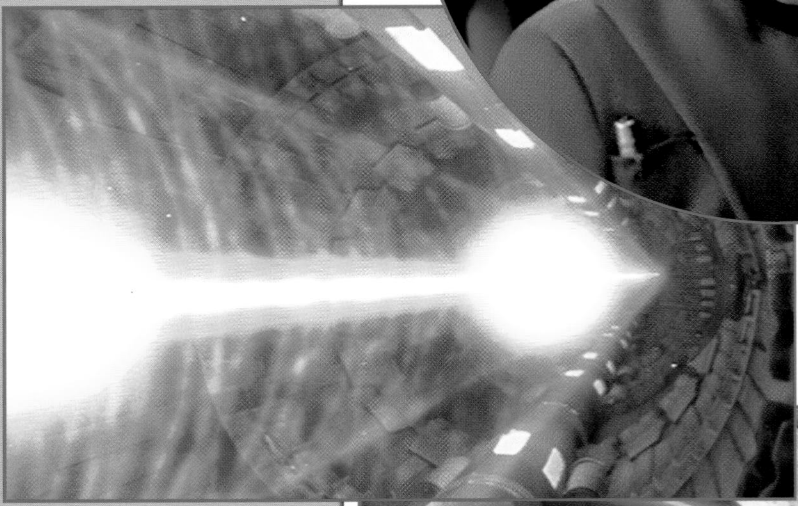

INTERIOR MILLENNIUM FALCON – COCKPIT

THE SHIP IS BUFFETED BY THE TREMENDOUS EXPLOSION OF THE REBEL CRUISER. LANDO AND HIS COPILOT ARE STUNNED BY THE SIGHT OF THE DEATH STAR FIREPOWER.

LANDO

That blast came from the Death Star! That thing's operational!

(INTO COMLINK)

Home One, this is Gold Leader.

INTERIOR REBEL STAR CRUISER – BRIDGE

ACKBAR STANDS AMID THE CONFUSION ON THE WIDE BRIDGE AND SPEAKS INTO THE COMLINK.

ACKBAR

We saw it. All craft prepare to retreat.

INTERIOR MILLENNIUM FALCON – COCKPIT

LANDO

You won't get another chance at this, Admiral.

INTERIOR REBEL STAR CRUISER – BRIDGE

ACKBAR

We have no choice, General Calrissian. Our cruisers can't repel firepower of that magnitude.

INTERIOR MILLENNIUM FALCON – COCKPIT

LANDO

Han will have that shield down. We've got to give him more time.

EXTERIOR FOREST – GENERATOR BUNKER

MEANWHILE, THE FOREST BATTLE IS RAGING, TOO.

THREEPIO

We're coming!

ARTOO AND THREEPIO MAKE IT TO THE DOOR, AS HAN AND LEIA PROVIDE COVER FIRE.

121

HAN

Come on! Come on!

THE LITTLE DROID MOVES TO THE
TERMINAL AND PLUGS IN HIS
COMPUTER ARM.

THREEPIO

Oh, Artoo, hurry!

A LARGE EXPLOSION HITS NEAR
ARTOO, KNOCKING HIM BACKWARDS.
THE STUBBY ASTRODROID'S HEAD IS
SMOLDERING. SUDDENLY, THERE IS A
LOUD SPROOING AND HAN AND LEIA
TURN AROUND TO SEE ARTOO WITH
ALL HIS COMPARTMENT DOORS OPEN,
AND ALL OF HIS APPENDAGES
STICKING OUT; WATER AND SMOKE
SPURT OUT OF THE NOZZLES IN HIS
BODY.

THREEPIO

My goodness! Artoo, why
did you have to be so
brave?

HAN

Well, I suppose I could
hotwire this thing.

    HAN TURNS TO THE
    TERMINAL.

    LEIA

    I'll cover you.

122

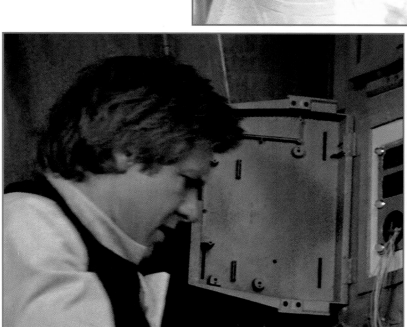

A WALKER LUMBERS FORWARD, SHOOTING LASER BLASTS AT FRANTIC EWOKS RUNNING IN ALL DIRECTIONS. TWO EWOKS ARE STRUCK DOWN BY LASER BLASTS. ONE TRIES TO AWAKEN HIS FRIEND, THEN REALIZES THAT HE IS DEAD.

EXTERIOR SPACE – DEATH STAR

THE REBEL FLEET CONTINUES TO BE PICKED OFF BY THE DEATH STAR'S DEADLY BEAM.

INTERIOR MILLENNIUM FALCON – COCKPIT

LANDO STEERS THE FALCON WILDLY THROUGH AN OBSTACLE COURSE OF FLOATING GIANTS. HE'S BEEN YELLING INTO THE COMLINK.

LANDO (DESPERATELY)

Yes! I said closer! Move as close as you can and engage those Star Destroyers at point-blank range.

INTERIOR REBEL STAR CRUISER – BRIDGE

ACKBAR

At that close range we won't last long against those Star Destroyers.

INTERIOR MILLENNIUM FALCON – COCKPIT

LANDO

We'll last longer than we will against that Death Star...and we might just take a few of them with us.

EXTERIOR SPACE
– IMPERIAL STAR DESTROYER

THE REBEL CRUISERS MOVE VERY CLOSE TO THE IMPERIAL STAR DESTROYERS AND BEGIN TO BLAST AWAY AT POINT-BLANK RANGE. TINY FIGHTERS RACE ACROSS THE GIANT SURFACES, AGAINST A BACKDROP OF LASER FIRE.

INTERIOR REBEL COCKPIT

REBEL PILOT

She's gonna blow!

EXTERIOR SPACE

THE CONTROL TOWER OF A STAR DESTROYER BLOWS UP.

INTERIOR REBEL Y-WING COCKPIT

Y-WING PILOT

I'm hit!

EXTERIOR SPACE – IMPERIAL STAR DESTROYER

THE DAMAGED Y-WING PLUMMETS TOWARDS A STAR DESTROYER, AND CRASHES INTO IT, EXPLODING.

124

INTERIOR EMPEROR'S TOWER — THRONE ROOM

Out of the window and on the viewscreens, the Rebel fleet is being decimated in blinding explosions of light and debris. But in here is no sound of battle. The Emperor speaks to Luke, and Vader watches him.

EMPEROR

Your fleet is lost. And your friends on the Endor moon will not survive. There is no escape, my young apprentice. The Alliance will die...as will your friends.

Luke's eyes are full of rage.

EMPEROR

Good. I can feel your anger. I am defenseless. Take your weapon! Strike me down with all of your hatred and your journey towards the dark side will be complete.

LUKE CAN RESIST NO LONGER. THE
LIGHTSABER FLIES INTO HIS HAND. HE
IGNITES IT IN AN INSTANT AND SWINGS AT
THE EMPEROR. VADER'S LIGHTSABER
FLASHES INTO VIEW, BLOCKING LUKE'S BLOW
BEFORE IT CAN REACH THE EMPEROR. THE
TWO BLADES SPARK AT CONTACT.

EXTERIOR
FOREST

THE
BATTLE
RAGES ON.

CHEWIE SWINGS
ON A VINE TO THE
ROOF OF ONE OF THE
WALKERS. TWO EWOKS CLING TO HIM.
THEY LAND WITH A THUD ON THE TOP
OF THE LURCHING MACHINE.

ONE OF THE EWOKS PEEKS THROUGH
THE WINDOW.

WALKER PILOT #1

Look!

WALKER PILOT #2

Get him off of there!

The walker pilot opens the hatch to see what's going on. He is yanked out and tossed overboard before he can scream. The two Ewoks jump into the cockpit and knock the second pilot unconscious. As the mighty machine careens out of control, outside Chewie is almost knocked overboard; he sticks his head into the hatch with a series of angry barks. The Ewoks are too busy and frightened to listen to the Wookiee's complaint. Chewie slips inside the walker.

Chewbacca's walker moves through the forest, destroying another Imperial walker, and firing laser blasts at unsuspecting stormtroopers. The Ewoks shout and cheer as the giant machine helps turn the tide of the battle in their favor.

A speeder bike chases Ewoks
through the underbush. As
the scout rounds a tree, he is
knocked off his bike by a vine
tied between two trees.

As a walker moves in, Ewoks
cut vines restraining two huge
logs that swing down and
smash the walker's head flat.

A walker marches through the
undergrowth blasting Ewoks
as it goes. An Ewok warrior
gives the signal, and a pile of
logs is cut loose. The logs
tumble under the walker's
feet, causing it to slip and
slide until it finally topples
over with a great crash.

A scout bike races past and is
lassoed with a heavy vine.

127

THE OTHER END OF THE VINE
IS TIED TO A TREE, AND THE
BIKE SWINGS AROUND IN EVER
TIGHTENING CIRCLES UNTIL IT
RUNS OUT OF ROPE AND
CRASHES INTO THE TREES WITH
A HUGE EXPLOSION.

EXTERIOR FOREST – GENERATOR
BUNKER

HAN WORKS FURIOUSLY AT THE
CONTROL PANEL AS HE
ATTEMPTS TO HOTWIRE THE
DOOR. LEIA IS COVERING HIM.

HAN

I think I got it. I got it!

AS THE CONNECTION IS MADE,
WITH LOUD SQUEAKS, A
SECOND DOOR SLIDES ACROSS
IN FRONT OF THE FIRST.

HAN FROWNS AND TURNS
BACK TO THE WIRES
AGAIN. LEIA SUDDENLY
CRIES OUT IN PAIN, HER
SHOULDER HIT BY A
LASER BLAST.

128

THREEPIO

Oh, Princess Leia, are you all right?

HAN

Let's see.

LEIA

It's not bad.

STORMTROOPER (OFFSCREEN)

Freeze!

THEY FREEZE.

THREEPIO

Oh, dear.

STORMTROOPER

Don't move!

LEIA HOLDS HER LASER GUN READY, BEHIND HAN, OUT OF VIEW OF THE TWO STORMTROOPERS MOVING TOWARD THEM. HAN AND LEIA'S EYES LOCK; THE MOMENT SEEMS SUSPENDED IN TIME.

HAN

I love you.

ANOTHER SHARED LOOK BETWEEN THEM, AS SHE SMILES UP AT HAN.

LEIA

I know.

STORMTROOPER

Hands up! Stand up!

129

HAN TURNS SLOWLY, REVEALING THE GUN IN LEIA'S HAND. SHE DISPOSES OF THE STORMTROOPERS IN A FLASH. AS HAN TURNS BACK TO LEIA, HE LOOKS UP TO SEE A GIANT WALKER APPROACH AND STAND BEFORE HIM, ITS DEADLY WEAPONS AIMED RIGHT AT HIM.

HAN (TO LEIA)

Stay back.

THE HATCH ON TOP OF THE WALKER OPENS AND CHEWIE STICKS HIS HEAD OUT AND BARKS TRIUMPHANTLY.

HAN

Chewie! Get down here! She's wounded! No, wait...I got an idea.

INTERIOR EMPEROR'S TOWER – THRONE ROOM

LUKE AND VADER ARE ENGAGED IN A MAN-TO-MAN DUEL OF LIGHTSABERS EVEN MORE VICIOUS THAN THE BATTLE ON BESPIN. BUT THE YOUNG JEDI HAS GROWN STRONGER IN THE INTERIM, AND NOW THE ADVANTAGE SHIFTS TO HIM. VADER IS FORCED BACK, LOSING HIS BALANCE, AND IS KNOCKED DOWN THE STAIRS.

131

LUKE STANDS AT THE
TOP OF THE STAIRS,
READY TO ATTACK.

EMPEROR
(LAUGHING)

Good. Use your aggressive
feelings, boy! Let the hate
flow through you.

LUKE LOOKS
MOMENTARILY BACK AT
THE EMPEROR, THEN
BACK TO VADER, AND
REALIZES HE IS USING
THE DARK SIDE. HE
TURNS OFF HIS
LIGHTSABER, AND
RELAXES, DRIVING THE
HATE FROM HIS BEING.

VADER

Obi-Wan has taught you
well.

LUKE

I will not fight you, Father.

VADER WALKS BACK UP
THE STAIRS TO LUKE.

VADER

You are unwise to lower
your defenses.

VADER ATTACKS,
FORCING LUKE ON THE
DEFENSIVE.

The young Jedi leaps in an amazing reverse flip up to the safety of the catwalk overhead. Vader stands below him.

LUKE

Your thoughts betray you, Father. I feel the good in you...the conflict.

VADER

There is no conflict.

LUKE

You couldn't bring yourself to kill me before and I don't believe you'll destroy me now.

VADER

You underestimate the power of the dark side. If you will not fight, then you will meet your destiny.

Vader throws the laser sword and it cuts through the supports holding the catwalk, then returns to Vader's hand.

LUKE TUMBLES TO THE GROUND IN A
SHOWER OF SPARKS AND ROLLS OUT OF
SIGHT UNDER THE EMPEROR'S PLATFORM.
VADER MOVES TO FIND HIM.

EMPEROR (LAUGHS)

Good. Good.

EXTERIOR SPACE – AIR BATTLE

THE TWO ARMADAS, LIKE THEIR SEA-BOUND
ANCESTORS, BLAST AWAY AT EACH OTHER IN
INDIVIDUAL POINT-BLANK CONFRONTATIONS.
THE FALCON AND SEVERAL FIGHTERS
ATTACK ONE OF THE LARGER IMPERIAL
SHIPS.

INTERIOR MILLENNIUM FALCON – COCKPIT

LANDO

Watch out. Squad at point oh-six.

INTERIOR REBEL COCKPIT

REBEL PILOT

I'm on it, Gold Leader.

INTERIOR WEDGE'S X-FIGHTER COCKPIT

WEDGE

Good shot, Red Two.

EXTERIOR SPACE

THE DOGFIGHT RAGES.

INTERIOR MILLENIUM FALCON – COCKPIT

LANDO

Now...come on, Han, old buddy. Don't let me down.

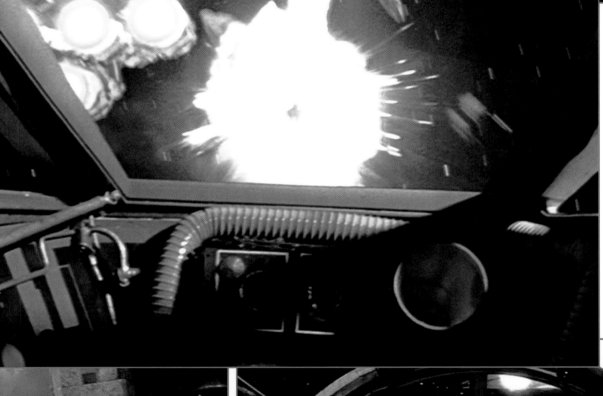

EXTERIOR FOREST – GENERATOR BUNKER

CHEWIE'S WALKER STANDS IN FRONT OF THE DOOR TO THE BUNKER.

INTERIOR BUNKER CONTROL ROOM

CONTROLLERS WATCH THE MAIN VIEWSCREEN ON WHICH A VAGUE FIGURE OF AN IMPERIAL WALKER PILOT CAN BE SEEN. THERE IS A GREAT DEAL OF STATIC AND INTERFERENCE.

HAN/PILOT (VOICE-OVER)

It's over, Commander. The Rebels have been routed. They're fleeing into the woods. We need reinforcements to continue the pursuit.

THE CONTROLLERS ARE DELIGHTED.

CONTROL ROOM COMMANDER

Send three squads to help. Open the back door.

SECOND COMMANDER

Sir.

EXTERIOR FOREST – GENERATOR BUNKER

AS THE DOOR TO THE BUNKER OPENS AND THE IMPERIAL TROOPS RUSH OUT, THEY'RE SURPRISED TO FIND THEMSELVES SURROUNDED BY REBELS, THEIR WEAPONS POINTED AT THEM. EWOKS HOLDING BOWS AND ARROWS APPEAR ON THE ROOF OF THE BUNKER.

INTERIOR BUNKER

HAN, CHEWIE AND SEVERAL TROOPS HAVE RUSHED INTO THE CONTROL ROOM AND PLANT EXPLOSIVE CHARGES ON THE CONTROL PANELS.

HAN

Throw me another charge.

136

INTERIOR EMPEROR'S
TOWER – THRONE ROOM

VADER STALKS THE LOW-CEILINGED AREA
ON THE LEVEL BELOW THE THRONE,
SEARCHING FOR LUKE IN THE SEMI-
DARKNESS, HIS LIGHTSABER HELD READY.

VADER

You cannot hide for ever, Luke.

LUKE

I will not fight you.

VADER

Give yourself to the dark side. It is the only way you
can save your friends.

LUKE SHUTS HIS EYES TIGHTLY, IN
ANGUISH.

VADER

Yes, your thoughts betray you. Your feelings for them
are strong. Especially for...

VADER STOPS AND SENSES SOMETHING.

VADER

Sister! So...you have a twin sister. Your feelings have
now betrayed her too. Obi-Wan was wise to hide her
from me. Now his failure is complete. If you will not
turn to the dark side, then perhaps she will.

LUKE IGNITES HIS LIGHTSABER AND
SCREAMS IN ANGER.

LUKE

No!

HE RUSHES AT HIS FATHER WITH A FRENZY
WE HAVE NOT SEEN BEFORE. SPARKS FLY AS
LUKE AND VADER FIGHT IN THE CRAMPED
AREA.

LUKE'S HATRED FORCES VADER TO RETREAT
OUT OF THE LOW AREA AND ACROSS A
BRIDGE OVERLOOKING A VAST ELEVATOR
SHAFT. EACH STROKE OF LUKE'S SWORD
DRIVES HIS FATHER
FURTHER TOWARD
DEFEAT.

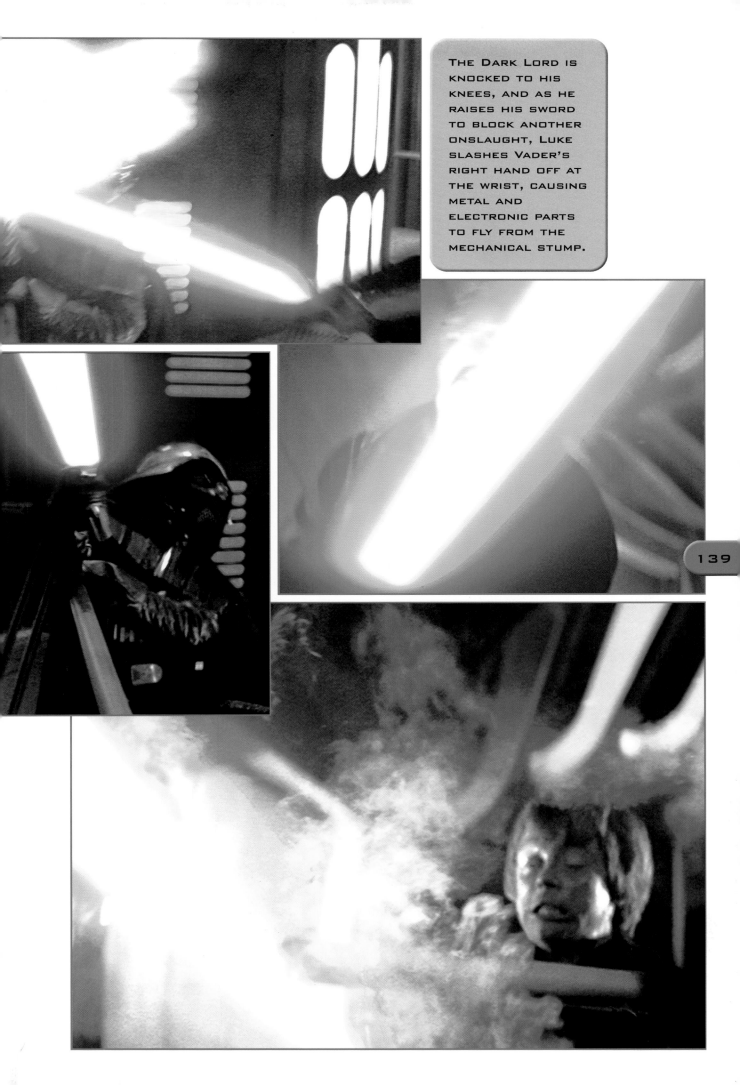

THE DARK LORD IS
KNOCKED TO HIS
KNEES, AND AS HE
RAISES HIS SWORD
TO BLOCK ANOTHER
ONSLAUGHT, LUKE
SLASHES VADER'S
RIGHT HAND OFF AT
THE WRIST, CAUSING
METAL AND
ELECTRONIC PARTS
TO FLY FROM THE
MECHANICAL STUMP.

139

VADER'S SWORD CLATTERS
USELESSLY AWAY, OVER THE EDGE
OF THE PLATFORM AND INTO THE
BOTTOMLESS SHAFT BELOW. LUKE
MOVES OVER VADER AND HOLDS
THE BLADE OF HIS SWORD TO THE
DARK LORD'S THROAT. THE
EMPEROR WATCHES WITH
UNCONTROLLABLE, PLEASED
AGITATION.

EMPEROR

**Good! Your hate has made you powerful.
Now, fulfill your destiny and take your
father's place at my side!**

LUKE LOOKS AT HIS FATHER'S
MECHANICAL HAND, THEN TO HIS
OWN MECHANICAL, BLACK-GLOVED
HAND, AND REALIZES HOW
MUCH HE IS BECOMING LIKE
HIS FATHER. HE MAKES THE
DECISION FOR WHICH HE HAS
SPENT A LIFETIME IN
PREPARATION.

Luke switches off his lightsaber.

LUKE

Never!

Luke casts his lightsaber away.

LUKE

I'll never turn to the dark side. You've failed, Your Highness. I am a Jedi, like my father before me.

The Emperor's glee turns to rage.

EMPEROR

So be it...Jedi.

EXTERIOR FOREST – GENERATOR BUNKER

Han and Rebel fighters run out of the bunker and race across the clearing.

HAN

Move! Move! Move!

The bunker explodes, followed by a spectacular display as the huge shield-generator radar dish explodes along with the bunker.

INTERIOR REBEL STAR CRUISER – BRIDGE

ACKBAR, SITTING IN HIS CONTROL CHAIR, SPEAKS INTO THE RADIO.

ACKBAR

The shield is down! Commence attack on the Death Star's main reactor.

INTERIOR MILLENNIUM FALCON – COCKPIT

LANDO

We're on our way. Red Group, Gold Group, all fighters follow me.

(LAUGHS)

Told you they'd do it!

EXTERIOR SPACE – DEATH STAR SURFACE

THE FALCON, FOLLOWED BY SEVERAL SMALLER REBEL FIGHTERS, HEADS TOWARD THE UNFINISHED SUPERSTRUCTURE OF THE DEATH STAR.

INTERIOR EMPEROR'S TOWER – THRONE ROOM

LUKE STANDS STILL, AS THE EMPEROR FACES HIM AT THE BOTTOM OF THE STAIRS.

EMPEROR

If you will not be turned, you will be destroyed.

THE EMPEROR RAISES HIS ARMS TOWARD LUKE. BLINDING BOLTS OF ENERGY, EVIL LIGHTNING, SHOOT FROM THE EMPEROR'S HANDS AT LUKE WITH SUCH SPEED AND POWER THE YOUNG JEDI SHRINKS BEFORE THEM, HIS KNEES BUCKLING.

THE WOUNDED VADER STRUGGLES TO HIS FEET, AND MOVES TO STAND AT HIS MASTER'S SIDE.

EMPEROR

Young fool...only now, at the end, do you understand.

LUKE IS ALMOST UNCONSCIOUS BENEATH THE CONTINUING ASSAULT OF THE EMPEROR'S LIGHTNING. HE CLUTCHES A CANISTER TO KEEP FROM FALLING INTO THE BOTTOMLESS SHAFT AS THE BOLTS TEAR THROUGH HIM.

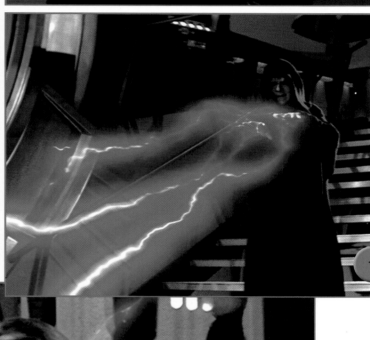

EMPEROR

Your feeble skills are no match for the power of the dark side. You have paid the price for your lack of vision.

LUKE WRITHES ON THE FLOOR IN UNBEARABLE PAIN, REACHING WEAKLY UP TOWARD WHERE VADER STANDS WATCHING.

LUKE (GROANS)

Father, please. Help me.

AGAIN, VADER STANDS, WATCHING LUKE. HE LOOKS AT HIS MASTER, THE EMPEROR, THEN BACK TO LUKE ON THE FLOOR.

EMPEROR

Now, young Skywalker...you will die.

ALTHOUGH IT WOULD NOT HAVE SEEMED POSSIBLE, THE OUTPOURING OF BOLTS FROM THE EMPEROR'S FINGERS ACTUALLY INCREASES IN INTENSITY, THE SOUND SCREAMING THROUGH THE ROOM. LUKE'S BODY WRITHES IN PAIN.

144

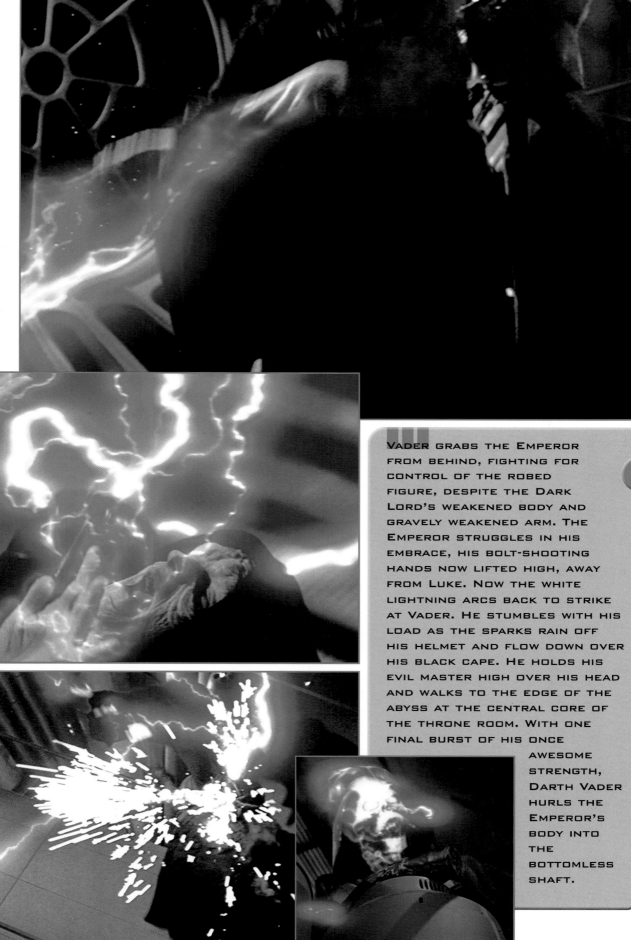

VADER GRABS THE EMPEROR FROM BEHIND, FIGHTING FOR CONTROL OF THE ROBED FIGURE, DESPITE THE DARK LORD'S WEAKENED BODY AND GRAVELY WEAKENED ARM. THE EMPEROR STRUGGLES IN HIS EMBRACE, HIS BOLT-SHOOTING HANDS NOW LIFTED HIGH, AWAY FROM LUKE. NOW THE WHITE LIGHTNING ARCS BACK TO STRIKE AT VADER. HE STUMBLES WITH HIS LOAD AS THE SPARKS RAIN OFF HIS HELMET AND FLOW DOWN OVER HIS BLACK CAPE. HE HOLDS HIS EVIL MASTER HIGH OVER HIS HEAD AND WALKS TO THE EDGE OF THE ABYSS AT THE CENTRAL CORE OF THE THRONE ROOM. WITH ONE FINAL BURST OF HIS ONCE AWESOME STRENGTH, DARTH VADER HURLS THE EMPEROR'S BODY INTO THE BOTTOMLESS SHAFT.

THE EMPEROR'S BODY SPINS HELPLESSLY
INTO THE VOID, ARCING AS IT FALLS INTO
THE ABYSS.

FINALLY, WHEN THE BODY IS FAR DOWN THE
SHAFT, IT EXPLODES, CREATING A RUSH OF
AIR THROUGH THE ROOM. VADER HAS
COLLAPSED BESIDE THE BOTTOMLESS HOLE.
LUKE CRAWLS TO HIS FATHER'S SIDE AND
PULLS HIM AWAY FROM THE EDGE OF THE
ABYSS TO SAFETY. BOTH THE YOUNG JEDI
AND THE GIANT WARRIOR ARE TOO WEAK TO
MOVE.

EXTERIOR/INTERIOR SPACE BATTLE
– FIGHTERS AND DEATH STAR

REBEL FIGHTERS ACCOMPANY THE FALCON
ACROSS THE SURFACE OF THE DEATH STAR
TO THE UNFINISHED PORTION, WHERE THEY
DIVE INTO THE SUPERSTRUCTURE OF THE
GIANT BATTLE STATION, FOLLOWED BY TIE
FIGHTERS.

WEDGE

I'm going in.

LANDO

Here goes nothing.

THE X-WING LEADS THE CHASE
THROUGH THE EVER-NARROWING
SHAFT, FOLLOWED BY THE FALCON
AND FOUR OTHER FIGHTERS, PLUS
TIE FIGHTERS WHO CONTINUALLY
FIRE AT THE REBELS.

LIGHTS REFLECT OFF THE PILOTS'
FACES AS THEY RACE THROUGH THE
DARK SHAFT.

LANDO

**Now lock onto the strongest power source. It
should be the power generator.**

WEDGE

**Form up. And stay alert. We could run out of
space real fast.**

THE FIGHTERS AND THE FALCON
RACE THROUGH THE TUNNEL, STILL
PURSUED BY THE TIE FIGHTERS.
ONE OF THE X-WINGS IS HIT FROM
BEHIND AND EXPLODES.

147

LANDO

Split up and head back to the surface. See if you can get a few of those TIE fighters to follow you.

PILOT

Copy, Gold Leader.

THE REBEL SHIPS PEEL OFF, PURSUED BY FOUR OF THE TIES, WHILE LANDO AND WEDGE CONTINUE THROUGH THE MAIN TUNNEL. IT NARROWS, AND THE FALCON SCRAPES THE SIDE DANGEROUSLY. TWO OTHER TIE FIGHTERS CONTINUE TO CHASE THEM.

LANDO

That was too close.

NIEN NUNB AGREES.

INTERIOR REBEL STAR CRUISER – BRIDGE

THE BATTLE BETWEEN THE REBEL AND IMPERIAL FLEETS RAGES ON.

ACKBAR

We've got to give those fighters more time. Concentrate all fire on that Super Star Destroyer.

EXTERIOR SPACE

REBEL CRAFT FIRE AT THE GIANT SUPER STAR DESTROYER.

148

INTERIOR VADER'S STAR
DESTROYER – BRIDGE

CONTROLLER

Sir, we've lost our bridge deflector shields.

ADMIRAL PIETT AND A COMMANDER
STAND AT THE WINDOW. THEY LOOK
CONCERNED.

PIETT

Intensify the forward batteries. I don't want
anything to get through.

EXTERIOR SPACE

OUTSIDE THE WINDOW A DAMAGED
REBEL FIGHTER IS OUT OF CONTROL AND
HEADING DIRECTLY TOWARD THE BRIDGE.

INTERIOR VADER'S STAR DESTROYER – BRIDGE

PIETT

Intensify forward firepower!

INTERIOR REBEL FIGHTER – COCKPIT

THE REBEL PILOT SCREAMS.

INTERIOR VADER'S STAR DESTROYER – BRIDGE

COMMANDER

Too late!

THE REBEL SHIP HITS THE STAR
DESTROYER, CAUSING A HUGE EXPLOSION.

EXTERIOR SPACE

THE GIANT BATTLESHIP LOSES CONTROL.

149

THERE IS EXCITEMENT ON THE BRIDGE AS THE BATTLE RAGES ON ALL SIDES. THEY CHEER AS THE GIANT STAR DESTROYER IS DESTROYED.

EXTERIOR SPACE – SURFACE OF THE DEATH STAR

THE GIANT STAR DESTROYER CRASHES INTO THE DEATH STAR AND EXPLODES.

INTERIOR DEATH STAR – MAIN DOCKING BAY

CHAOS. FOR THE FIRST TIME, THE DEATH STAR IS ROCKED BY EXPLOSIONS AS THE REBEL FLEET, NO LONGER BACKED AGAINST A WALL, ZOOMS OVER, UNLOADING A HEAVY BARRAGE. IMPERIAL TROOPS RUN IN ALL DIRECTIONS, CONFUSED AND DESPERATE TO ESCAPE.

IN THE MIDST OF THIS UPROAR, LUKE IS TRYING TO CARRY THE ENORMOUS DEADWEIGHT OF HIS FATHER'S WEAKENING BODY TOWARD AN IMPERIAL SHUTTLE. FINALLY, LUKE COLLAPSES FROM THE STRAIN. THE EXPLOSIONS GROW LOUDER AS VADER DRAWS HIM CLOSER.

VADER

Luke, help me take this mask off.

LUKE

But you'll die.

VADER

Nothing can stop that now. Just for once let me look on you with my own eyes.

SLOWLY, HESITANTLY, LUKE REMOVES THE MASK FROM HIS FATHER'S FACE. THERE BENEATH THE SCARS IS AN ELDERLY MAN. HIS EYES DO NOT FOCUS. BUT THE DYING MAN SMILES AT THE SIGHT BEFORE HIM.

ANAKIN (VERY WEAK)

Now...go, my son. Leave me.

LUKE

No. You're coming with me. I'll not leave you here. I've got to save you.

ANAKIN

You already have, Luke. You were right. You were right about me. Tell your sister...you were right.

LUKE

Father...I won't leave you.

DARTH VADER, ANAKIN SKYWALKER...LUKE'S FATHER DIES.

EXTERIOR DEATH STAR

A LONE X-WING IS JUST IN FRONT OF THE MILLENNIUM FALCON ON ITS SWERVING BOMB RUN THROUGH THE IMMENSE SUPERSTRUCTURE OF THE HALF-BUILT DEATH STAR. THEY ARE PURSUED BY TIE FIGHTERS.

INTERIOR WEDGE'S X-FIGHTER – COCKPIT

WEDGE

There it is!

EXTERIOR DEATH STAR

THE REBELS HOME IN ON THE MAIN REACTOR SHAFT. IT IS AWESOME.

INTERIOR FALCON COCKPIT

LANDO

All right, Wedge. Go for the power regulator on the north tower.

INTERIOR WEDGE'S X-FIGHTER – COCKPIT

WEDGE

Copy, Gold Leader. I'm already on my way out.

EXTERIOR DEATH STAR

THE X-WING HEADS FOR THE TOP OF THE HUGE REACTOR AND FIRES SEVERAL PROTON TORPEDOES AT THE POWER REGULATOR, CAUSING A SERIES OF SMALL EXPLOSIONS.

THE FALCON HEADS FOR THE MAIN
REACTOR, AND LANDO FIRES THE MISSILES,
WHICH SHOOT OUT OF THE FALCON WITH A
POWERFUL ROAR, AND HIT DIRECTLY AT THE
CENTER OF THE MAIN REACTOR.

INTERIOR FALCON COCKPIT

LANDO WINCES AT THE DANGEROUSLY CLOSE
EXPLOSION.

EXTERIOR DEATH STAR

HE MANEUVERS THE FALCON OUT OF THE
WINDING SUPERSTRUCTURE JUST AHEAD OF
THE CONTINUING CHAIN OF EXPLOSIONS.

INTERIOR REBEL STAR CRUISER

ACKBAR LEANS ON THE RAILING OF THE
BRIDGE, WATCHING THE LARGE SCREEN
SHOWING THE DEATH STAR IN THE MAIN
BRIEFING ROOM.

ACKBAR

Move the fleet away from the Death Star.

EXTERIOR/INTERIOR DEATH STAR
– IMPERIAL SHUTTLE

AN IMPERIAL SHUTTLE, WITH LUKE AT THE
CONTROLS, ROCKETS OUT OF THE MAIN
DOCKING BAY AS THAT ENTIRE SECTION OF
THE DEATH STAR IS BLOWN AWAY.

INTERIOR WEDGE'S X-FIGHTER – COCKPIT

WEDGE IS RELIEVED TO ESCAPE THE DEATH
STAR.

153

EXTERIOR/INTERIOR DEATH STAR – FALCON COCKPIT

FINALLY, JUST AS IT LOOKS LIKE THE FALCON
WILL NOT MAKE IT, LANDO EXPERTLY PILOTS
THE CRAFT OUT OF THE EXPLODING
SUPERSTRUCTURE AND WHIZZES TOWARD THE
SANCTUARY MOON, ONLY A MOMENT BEFORE
THE DEATH STAR SUPER-NOVAS INTO OBLIVION.

INTERIOR MILLENNIUM FALCON – COCKPIT

LANDO AND NIEN NUNB LAUGH AND CHEER
IN RELIEF.

EXTERIOR SPACE

THE DEATH STAR SUPER-NOVAS INTO
OBLIVION BEHIND THE FALCON.

EXTERIOR ENDOR FOREST

HAN AND LEIA, CHEWIE, THE DROIDS, THE
REBEL TROOPS AND THE EWOKS ALL LOOK
TO THE SKY AS THE DEATH STAR REVEALS
ITSELF IN A FINAL FLASH OF
SELF-DESTRUCTION. THEY ALL CHEER.

THREEPIO

They did it!

HAN LOOKS DOWN FROM THE SKY TO LEIA,
A LOOK OF CONCERN ON HIS FACE. LEIA
CONTINUES TO LOOK AT THE SKY AS
THOUGH LISTENING FOR A SILENT VOICE.

HAN

I'm sure Luke wasn't on that thing when it blew.

LEIA

He wasn't. I can feel it.

HAN

You love him, don't you?

LEIA SMILES, PUZZLED.

LEIA

Yes.

HAN

All right. I understand. Fine. When he comes back, I won't get in the way.

SHE REALIZES HIS MISUNDERSTANDING.

LEIA

Oh. No, it's not like that at all. He's my brother.

HAN IS STUNNED BY THIS NEWS. SHE SMILES, AND THEY EMBRACE.

156

EXTERIOR ENDOR FOREST – NIGHT

LUKE SETS A TORCH TO THE LOGS STACKED UNDER A FUNERAL PYRE WHERE HIS FATHER'S ARMOR LIES: BLACK MASK, HELMET AND CAPE. HE STANDS WATCHING SADLY AS THE FLAMES LEAP HIGHER TO CONSUME WHAT'S LEFT OF VADER.

In the sky above, fireworks explode and Rebel fighters zoom above the forest.

EXTERIOR CLOUD CITY – SUNSET

Fireworks explode above the city as searchlights pan the sky. A twin-pod cloud car zooms in above the festivities.

EXTERIOR TATOOINE – DAY

A skyhopper weaves around buildings as confetti falls over the city, awash in celebration.

EXTERIOR CORUSCANT PLAZA – NIGHT

Confetti falls on the city as hundreds of citizens celebrate. An airspeeder flies overhead. Fireworks explode in the full-moon sky.

EXTERIOR EWOK VILLAGE SQUARE – NIGHT

A huge bonfire is the centerpiece of a wild celebration. Rebels and Ewoks rejoice in the warm glow of firelight, drums beating, singing, dancing, and laughing in the communal language of victory and liberation.

LANDO RUNS IN AND IS
ENTHUSIASTICALLY HUGGED BY
HAN AND CHEWIE. THEN,
FINALLY, LUKE ARRIVES AND THE
FRIENDS RUSH TO GREET AND
EMBRACE HIM.

THEY STAND CLOSE, THIS HARDY
GROUP, TAKING COMFORT IN
EACH OTHER'S TOUCH,
TOGETHER TO THE END.

Rebels and Ewoks join together in dancing and celebration. The original group of adventurers watches from the sidelines. Only Luke seems distracted, alone in their midst, his thoughts elsewhere.

159

HE LOOKS OFF TO THE SIDE AND SEES
THREE SHIMMERING, SMILING FIGURES AT
THE EDGE OF THE SHADOWS: BEN KENOBI,
YODA, AND ANAKIN SKYWALKER.

FADE OUT

END CREDITS OVER STAR FIELD

THE END